D1622127

THE
FINANCIAL AFTERMATH
OF WAR

THE
FINANCIAL AFTERMATH
OF WAR

By
SIR JOSIAH STAMP
G.B.E., LL.D., D.SC., F.B.A.

LONDON
ERNEST BENN LIMITED

First Published in

I 9 3 2

Printed

in

Great Britain

TO

THE MEMORY OF

ABERYSTWYTH DAYS

OF 1899

CONTENTS

PREFACE

A short vacation in 1930 at Aberystwyth provided, or provoked, the occasion for giving five lectures, on successive evenings, in the University, and reasons of sentiment completed the impulse. The lectures were included in a special series, to which was attached an obligation to publish, but for which I should have been reluctant to pass them into print. For they were only an attempt to express to students without any economic knowledge or previous interest, and to the general public who attended in gratifying numbers, in the simplest and most elementary terms I could command, the chief facts and considerations about post-war finance. They claim no merit whatever for the experienced student —and are indeed in places simplified or symbolised to an extent which must be painful to him—but I hope that many people, alike in outlook to those who heard them, may now read them with some advantage. I also hope that they may be useful in the higher forms of schools, where to an increasing extent the elementary economics of public affairs are being studied, but for which suitable books are scarce. The lectures have been reproduced here practically as delivered—apart from touches of local colour and jests already *démodé*—but with the addition of a few recent facts, and of a broadcast address upon the gold standard.

J. C. S.

SHORTLANDS, KENT.
February 1932.

I

Some Definitions

The subject we are to consider lies, of course,
mainly in the field of economics, or, very literally, what used to be called Political Economy.
But it also lies in the field of Social Psychology,
and again, to a considerable extent, in the field
of Political Institutions. It obviously lies in the
field of economics, because it affects the production, distribution and consumption of wealth.
To a most important extent it involves distribution, not so much in putting wealth where consumers want it, but rather in the sense of divid-
ing wealth up amongst different classes of people.
You may remember the schoolboy's definition
recently of political economy as " the thing that
tells you how to get what you want with the
minimum honest effort." Now, whatever we may
think of that as a definition of the science, it is
most certainly a true description of the way in
which people get their ideas of economics. They
are prepared to regard with awe the discipline
required to become chemists or physicists or
linguists or doctors, but they spring fully fledged
into economists by holding quite positive views
on the most intricate economic problems with
the minimum honest effort. It is always difficult

to convince them that an intellectual discipline at least equal to that demanded in the other sciences is also required for this, and that, in addition, it compels a discipline of the spirit that is of the will and of partisanship, which many never successfully undergo.

This subject lies in the field of economics, not only on the intellectual side, but on the side of temperament, and it will raise many issues that will start your prejudices and appeal to your likes and dislikes, calling upon you for self-restraint in a way that is foreign to other subjects. When it is said that the subject lies also in the field of social psychology, we mean that it has to discover how people react to different events. The social psychology of France, Germany and Great Britain respectively will differ to an extent which will make the results of a similar set of circumstances widely divergent. The people respond differently to the pressure of hope and of fear and of social appeal. Moreover, different classes of society also react differently to the same stimulus, and the same class will react differently at different periods. In the third place, the subject touches that of political institutions because what *ought* to be done, what *can* be done and what *will* be done, as a result of particular events, must always depend upon the machinery available, upon its administrative strength and its political background. There has been, for example, an immense difference in the promptness with which a particular financial situation has been met by the machinery of direct taxation in England, France and Germany —in the case of France, because of a much younger and less well-equipped administrative machine; in the case of Germany, because of the historical division of the field of taxation between central Government, or the Reich, the separate States, such as Prussia and Saxony, and the local Communes. No one can really understand the differences in the financial aftermath of war in different countries without a knowledge of their political institutions.

The Object in View

The broad purpose of these lectures is to give a general background to present events and the story that will be gradually unfolded during the lifetime of all the younger members of this audience. While I want you to be interested in past history, my main object is to give you a key to the unfolding economic life. Remember that most political events to-day, quite unlike the past, when they had their roots in rival dynasties, in religious differences and in questions of political representation, are economic—they are bound up with the production and distribution of wealth. Most of the other great problems that vexed our fathers are now in the background. It is true we have Empire problems, but such burning questions as the Reform Bill, Catholic Emancipation, etc., have only an historical interest. If most political events to-day are economic, then we can also say that most economic questions are financial as well ; that is to say, they have a financial façade. Nothing financial is really final; it has an economic reality behind it. It is only a monetary expression of something much more real than money, and yet it is often the only way in which we can measure and study the economic. If then most economic questions are financial, we can quite truly say to-day that most financial questions are affected by what happened during the war, and what has happened in consequence since. It is not my desire to give you a complete compendium of information on the various subjects with which I deal, for there are many books to which you can refer if you want quantities of information. Nor do I desire to give you masses of statistics, and these will be kept down to the very minimum necessary to illustrate principles and tendencies. The object is to suggest lines of study and reading, and, most of all, to stimulate in you a " mode of thought " about these questions which is not normal to human thinking until it has been started and encouraged. There is much in what will be said that you will not find exactly in book form anywhere else, though you can supplement and correct by reference to recognised authorities.

The Personal Element

I am going to apologise at the outset for the many personal elements that you will find—this

will save me interjecting at every point where
I draw on my own experience or memory for
matters not on record, and with a purely personal point of view. In order that the younger
students should not be puzzled by some of my
references, let me explain outright that throughout the war I was personally engaged in the chief
constructive and administrative changes connected with the vast increases of taxation that
the war necessitated. I frequently assisted the
several Chancellors in connection with the in-
come-tax legislation, particularly the questions
that arose through double taxation in different
parts of the Empire. I was one of the framers of
the scheme of Excess Profits Duty, and saw it
right through its legislative and administrative
history. Special levies on munitions establish-
ments and particularly upon the small remaining
profits of the coal mines, the new and short-lived
taxes upon corporations, came within my personal knowledge ; and service on a Committee
during the war to deal with the problems that
would arise when an anticipated slump in prices
came at the end of the war, and all the financial
risks that were involved, was valuable to me.
Mention must be made of the Committee (under
the auspices of the League of Nations) that led off
on Double Taxation throughout the world ; the
Royal Commission on Income Tax, which led to
the revision of the whole of that great historical
scheme in the light of modern times ; the Committee on the Taxation of War Wealth ; the

division of the taxation revenues and burdens between England and Northern Ireland after the separation of their exchequers ; and the work of the Colwyn Committee in discussing the National Debt and Taxation, which gave much consideration to the proposal for a capital levy. I had some personal connection, too, on Government Commissions and Committees, with official consideration of the re-establishment of the gold standard and its effects. In the " Dawes " Committee on German Reparations in 1924, in reports to the International Chamber of Commerce, and in the " Young Committee " in 1929, there was enough experience of international complexities of this aspect of the aftermath of war to last me a lifetime. I mention these things, not as an egotistic record, but only to save me interjecting at innumerable points where personal questions are involved, and perhaps to give you some little idea of the continuous series of fumblings and grapplings with financial riddles which the war has entailed.

The Ground to be Covered

I am to speak on the aftermath of war. It will mostly be this Great War, but of course reference will be made also occasionally to the Napoleonic and the Franco-Prussian Wars. The matters discussed will relate mostly to Great Britain, but I shall also have to deal with France, Germany and the United States, in order that the interworking of their finance with ours may

be understood. So that you may get a more
general and less particular view of some aspects
of the aftermath, I have divided the series under
five titles, which will serve in the main as subjects
for each lecture. But you must not imagine that
they are clearly defined and quite separate—we
shall sometimes have to anticipate something
that is dealt with later in detail ; at other times
we shall come back on our tracks to pick up a
lesson from the previous lecture. You must see
the picture as a whole, though we shall have to
study it in sections, and sometimes work backwards or forwards, but the separate subjects have
this in common, that they are interlaced and
inter-related, and they all make special problems
for society and for industry. All of them are
going to affect the life of everyone of you probably throughout its whole course, either obviously or unconsciously, and, therefore, there is
nothing academic or merely theoretical about
them. If we are to get far upon this subject, we
must not be the slaves of words or the servants
of opinion. Above all, a *realistic* picture of what
is really happening is necessary. If your minds
and mine are to work together to a common realisation of the problem, we must have an understanding about many matters straightaway.
You have to realise that what we are discussing
are not merely so many figures in so many
ledgers ; strictly, we are not studying figures at
all—we are studying who is to make, and who is
to possess, all kinds of foods, boots, hats, dresses

2

and other good things on which our lives, however ethereal we may be, so greatly depend. I might very well have called this series by a different title, viz. " The Struggle for the National Product."

The National Heap

To get this realistic picture, I propose to adopt a figure found to be helpful on previous occasions, and which will be referred to again and again until you have achieved the only vital method of thinking on the problem. You must think of all the things that are done by the people of these islands every year—of the manual work in producing articles for use and consumption, the mental product of authors, of preachers in sermons and professors in lectures, of all that results from the abstinence and thrift of past years in the machinery and factories which so greatly help our minds and muscles in producing wealth. I want you to imagine all these products heaped together in one vast quantity in this hall, just as if we had vehicles bringing them in and piling them up. There will be added to the heap we make, products from other lands, many foodstuffs, and a balance of production which is due to us for all we have done abroad in lending money in centuries gone by. There is the great heap, and our economic life really consists of piling it up and then taking it away in different lots. Those who put on one thing take away another, and there are certain rules and regulations, brought about partly by natural economic processes and partly by social convention, which decide what each person is entitled to take off it. When they put their contributions on, they are given certain " tickets " or " vouchers " entitling them to take something away, and we want to realise first of all that the total number of vouchers and tickets, or what is " authorised " upon them, will just suffice, when they are handed in to the storekeeper, to clear away the whole heap—in other words, they are equal in total " value " or contents to the total heap. Obviously they must be, just as all the tickets issued by a cloakroom as claims on the contents represent neither more nor less than those contents.

Let us look at some of the people who are entitled to come up with their tickets, or money, to take something off the heap. First of all there are the civil servants of various kinds. It is only by their efforts that the heap has been kept as large as it is, for they have either been active in a regulating or organising capacity, preventing muddle, or they have been the keepers of the peace, and have enabled us, working in security from molestation, to make our contributions to the heap all the greater. When the tickets are given out to individuals the Government take some from each, which we then call " taxation," and they use the proceeds to hand over tickets to their civil servants entitling those servants to take a corresponding share of the heap.

They may have added nothing physical directly to the heap, but by their attentions others have made it bigger. Then there are the people who have lent money to productive enterprise in the past and are now entitled to draw interest. The heap is only as large as it is because of their assistance. They might very well have consumed their share in the past, but instead of doing so they " saved "; that is to say, they were responsible for a demand for bricks and materials which they could not consume instead of for cinemas, tobacco and all kinds of usable commodities. We need not go into the question as to the relative merits of their titles to the heap ; all that we need see now is that unless people were prepared to give them a share of future heaps, no one would go to the trouble of saving and going without, and there would be no capital aids to production. Now, it may well be that the community as a whole through the Government has done the borrowing, instead of individuals, and in that case the tickets are extracted by the Government as taxation and handed over to the people entitled to the interest, who then come to the heap for the commodities they desire. If we borrow money from abroad, then it is the foreigner who is entitled to come and either take his share of the heap or else re-lend it to the rest of us on promise of payment in the future. What must be remembered clearly is that the *size* of the heap does not depend merely upon those who are *directly producing* for it, but also upon a multitude of others who are looking after the producers, even amusing them, teaching them.

The Effect of War

Now consider what happens on the outbreak of war. First of all, a great many people who had been producers, who had been adding to it or helping others to add to it, have to go away and no longer put anything on the heap—they are fighting or helping others to fight, but they have to be kept in food and clothing all the same, and their " keep " comes off the heap. That is to say, it comes from other people's production. There is less then for everybody to consume by the amount that the old producers are no longer adding to the heap. The more people that go to the war, the smaller the national production—the more the heap shrinks. In the second place, the heap changes in its type. Many people who were producing luxuries and things that in hard times we can do without, begin to produce things that are required for war—clothing, boots, all kinds of munitions. So we find that the heap changes in its character. As the war goes on it becomes more and more a production specially for war uses, and many factories are empty that would put upon the heap purely peace luxuries, till what is left upon it is barely enough to keep people alive and clothed. But at that point a great number of new additions not known in peace-time begin to come about, and we find that the heap is kept up in the most surprising way. First, for example, women who did not add anything to the general exchangeable production— they may have done useful or useless work at home—begin to go out to work or begin to add in some other way to the general fund of services for other people. Idle daughters become munition workers. Everyone does his bit. People who were too old to work previously come back to work, or young people who would not otherwise have gone to work begin earlier, and the whole community begin to work overtime. By more people, young and old, at work, and by longer hours, in various ways we have a considerable number of additions.

Then secondly, in order to make the heap go as far as possible for *keeping* people, as distinct from giving them a good time, we have an addition to what are called " savings." People economise as far as possible, which means they take as little off the heap for their own consumption as they can, in order that others not adding that kind of thing may have more. They are not adding luxuries, they are adding, as far as possible, necessities, and when the war gets to an extreme point " rationing " sets in, so that the heap, restricted as it is, is made to go as far as possible in keeping men alive. In other words, there are fewer deductions from the heap. But even with all these efforts the time may come when perhaps the heap is not big enough to support all the people who are no longer adding to it. So thirdly, there comes a point when we borrow abroad, by

which we get additions of goods to the heap
from other people who are not drawing from the
heap themselves, just on the promise that some
day, perhaps fifty years after the war is over,
they shall have a special title to a repayment
from the national heap of that time and for
interest each year in the meantime. There is a
fourth expedient. Perhaps, instead of borrowing,
those who have been entitled to interest from
abroad which has been added to the heap from
the heaps of other nations, now *sell their securities*
and their title to the goods from abroad. This
means that they may have the equivalent of
that sale added to the heap immediately, and
instead of small annual additions for a long time
they have one very large addition at once.
Another and fifth method of making the heap go
a long way is to neglect to repair buildings and
machinery so long as they will do their work.
Repainting is allowed to stand over for a longer
period. People wear their suits and hats longer,
and thus they make less demands for new
things because they use the old longer. Thus
the heap, so diminished, in size by the absence
of producers, and in things usable for living
because of the production devoted to war
material, is kept up by new workers, overtime,
saving, borrowing and delayed renewals.

The Government's Task

Now, it is the collective will of the people—the
Government—who are carrying on the war, and

it is they who have to find a way of extracting products from the heap in order to keep the soldiers in food and in munitions of war. They have to get hold of the tickets for it somehow in order that the storekeeper will pass goods out to them and not to you or to me. The first way in which they get their tickets is by taxation, in which we are all specifically asked to give up tickets of title to the heap. This method has distinct limits. First of all, it has physical limits, because we must retain enough tickets ourselves to keep body and soul together. But long before this point is reached it has the psychological limit in its influence upon people's willingness to work and to add to the heap. Some taxation is " direct," like income tax, where the ticket is given up straightaway to the collector. Other taxation is " indirect," where a man is required to give up two tickets for a pint of beer or a pound of sugar instead of one, and the store-keeper hands over the extra ticket to the Government. Here it is open to the man to escape the tax by not buying the beer or tobacco, or sugar or tea, which is subject to duty.

The second method that the Government have of getting tickets is to borrow them, and to promise that there shall be returned out of future heaps interest, and ultimately repayment. You will have the right, by forgoing particular commodities off the heap this year, to have commodities in future years from future heaps. But the third way that the Government have to get hold of tickets is to print them themselves, and here tickets are not obtained from the people at all. They can do this in the night, as it were, without saying anything to anyone. Now, obviously, if there were just enough tickets before to correspond to the amount of goods, and a supply of new ones creeps in surreptitiously, the storekeeper will find that the whole of the heap is not exchanged for the whole of the tickets unless more tickets are given for each unit of goods. No one finds this out at once—gradually it becomes known that if you want to secure your goods from the heap, as there are a lot of tickets still not exchanged, you must come early and you must probably offer a little more than the so many tickets that you have given usually for a particular commodity if you really want to secure anything ; in other words, the printing of tickets more than the equivalent of the goods leads to the putting up of prices. It is the inevitable result of having more " purchasing power " in the tickets than there are goods to be bought. That is what is called Inflation. It is a hidden form of taxation, because for a given ticket you obtain less of the commodity than you did before. But do remember that the principle is that the tickets as a whole must be exchanged for the goods as a whole. I will deal with deflation another time ; it does not happen during the war. But inflation is the invariable accompaniment of war, and we shall have to say much about it.

The Similarity of Taxation and Borrowing

Now, you can only fight a war by the services
and commodities produced during the war or
existing at the outset. There is no such thing as
" throwing the burden on posterity," as you so
often hear, or " making posterity pay for the
war "—not in the sense that you can escape
from the actual production of all the goods at
the time.

Apart from their psychology, borrowing and
taxation are interchangeable ; there is no external difference between the immediate effect of
borrowing and taxation. They both mean that
there are fewer tickets, and so fewer goods, for the
taxed person or for the lender to consume. Of
course, if the borrowing is afterwards repudiated
and no repayment ever takes place, then it is the
same as though a very unfair and inconvenient
taxation had been applied at the time. But the
division of the Government's task between the
two methods is very important in its effect upon
the aftermath of war finance. While it is literally
true that you are unable to put the cost of war
on posterity, there is one sense in which it is only
partly true. War must, indeed, be fought on current efforts—on the bullets that are made to-day
and not on those made in the years to come. But
as between different *sections* of the people entitled
to take their share of the heap it is to some extent
not true, for if what might otherwise have been
taken from me as taxation is actually taken

as borrowed money, then other people are going to be taxed in the future more than they would otherwise have been, and my descendants will get more than they otherwise would have done. Therefore, taxation and borrowing really have a difference in the future rather than at the time.

The Proportion of War Expense borne by Taxes

There is one small school of thought in every war who think that the whole cost of the war should be raised by taxation. They say, in effect, the goods are taken away ; there is no external difference, and so there should only be the one claim made—that upon the taxpayer. There are others who go to the opposite extreme, and say that the Government should borrow all they want. We need not bother about these extremes, for the majority of people occupy a position somewhere between them, and the great point is to study the different positions they take up.

There were several principles actually in force during the war. The main principle in this country was to secure a balance between the two methods, and that the Government should put on enough *permanent* taxation to meet the permanent extra charges for interest and sinking funds after the war. In addition to that, they should get as much in special war taxes as possible, for this lessened the borrowing and therefore the permanent taxation required.

Each Chancellor, then, was eager to say in his budget that apart from special war taxes he had put on enough permanent taxes to give a yield after the war equal to the interest (and perhaps the sinking fund charges) on the borrowed money. Here, then, you have a kind of natural equation between borrowing and taxation. The French, if not avowedly, actually worked on the basis of borrowing and inflation. They did not believe in very heavy taxation during the war, and, as a matter of fact, they had no good machinery for raising direct taxes. What machinery they had was seriously interfered with in its man-power owing to war conditions, and a good part of their territory was in the hands of the enemy. The principle that animated the Germans, and kept up their spirits, was expressed: " We shall get such an indemnity from the defeated enemy that we need only borrow," and they too avoided heavy taxation.

Special Problems at the Beginning of War

Now, the first instinct in taxation when a war breaks out is to extend along the familiar lines— to impose some extra income tax or supertax, a little extra on beer or tea duties. " Business as usual " was the slogan in this country. Soon, however, special features crept into the taxing system—an extra number of estates came within the fiscal machine owing to the many deaths caused by the war, and special regulations about death duties not being too directly applied to such estates had to be passed. Then there follows a complete redistribution of the population and a great number assembling in particular parts, affecting such matters as public-house licences and customs regulations. It becomes a very active question whether the extra burden should be imposed upon the incomes (income tax) or the spending (in tobacco duties) of the soldiers who are fighting, or other people who are actively engaged in the war. There is an instinctive feeling that such people should not suffer the burdens that are falling on civilians. All kinds of changes begin to take place in commerce. Profits in many businesses go down, very likely, though not always, in luxuries. There is a special demand in other directions which creates special profits, so that we begin to hear of the special profits that are being made "owing to the war." Soon after the outbreak of the Great War one or two very special cases came to notice, particularly of flour millers, and the famous case of Spillers & Bakers so aroused public attention that there was an immediate outcry for taxing profits " that were due to the war." This idea is very obvious in the case of food-stuffs, which in view of short supply or anticipated difficulty in imports are quickly raised in price. It is also obvious in the special manufacture of munitions and clothes or uniforms in great quantities, and also very clear in cases of localities where there is a vast increase in the population, and therefore in easily made new profits in the shops. So at the end of 1914 and early in 1915 the old fortunes of the population began to be seriously changed ; the number of ups and downs were very remarkable. Some people were nearly destitute because their businesses had gone ; others had a certain new affluence. The desire to tax profits " due to the war " spread rapidly ; it became more and more obvious as time went on that it was impossible to draw a line and say what was distinctly *due* to the war. It fell to my lot to take part in framing a scheme of taxation designed to touch these special profits. It became obvious to us, how-ever, that the principle of " due to war " was not a practicable taxing expedient, and a new and different principle was substituted, which I might call the " better off " principle, i.e. that people were *lucky* who for any circumstances at all had an income greater than they had before the war, when everyone else was suffering. So without asking how the income arose, whether from harder work or from luck, whether it would have happened in any case, or whether from actual war activities—if, in fact, the income of the war period was higher than the pre-war income or standard,—then it was regarded as a " windfall " and as such specially or peculiarly liable to bear the special burdens of the war finance.

Taxation of Extra Profits

The history of the Excess Profits Duty is too intricate, interesting though it may be, to tell in this lecture. It was obviously necessary to provide for some " levelling " process ; so that if a concern or a business made a very high special profit in one year but a very low profit in the next, it should not pay more than another that had made the same amount of profit for the two years taken together, but in a different form ; different periods had to be merged. At the same time as the process of excess profits was going on there was important inflation taking place, and profits were more easily made in consequence.

In fact, they were not entirely merged on the amount of profits, but they were merged on the amount of duty payable, so that it was quite possible for one business to make an excess profit of £10,000 over two periods, and to pay an amount and rate of duty quite different from another concern which had made a similar amount for the two years, but differently distributed in those years. It is obvious that people who were making goods which were in much greater demand, even if their price did not rise, made larger profits—their output was greater. In other cases, although the sales might be less, scarcity drove prices very high and the net profit was greater. Excess profits were thus due to either output or price, or both. But very soon

an additional cause was at work, viz. general
inflation. Prices rose all round, even for commodities that were not reduced in supply or
specially increased in demand. (I shall have
occasion to refer to this in dealing with inflation
later on.) During the course of the war a comparison of the activities of any business with its
pre-war results produced an apparent excess,
because all the goods sold were expressed in
higher amounts of currency—in more tickets, so
to speak. Whenever this happens it has an
important effect upon the incidence of taxation,
because the profit of any particular year is
swollen by the automatic increase in prices upon
the stock that has been sold, and if the price has
to fall again at some later period, the profits of
that later year will be reduced, or losses will be
made, owing to the price of sale either falling
below the price of purchase, or reducing the
customary margin between them. In the later
years of the war, when huge sums were being paid
in Excess Profits Duty, it was the custom to
allege that these were " paper profits " because
of the loss anticipated when prices should fall
again. Elaborate provisions were therefore
made for dealing with this situation after the
Excess Profits Duty had come to an end. As a
matter of fact, the duty was not taken off at the
end of the war, but ran on two whole years, and
the collapse of prices came before the duty was
repealed. The collapse brought about very bad
results for traders in the last year of the duty ;

it gave him the right, with his losses and deficiencies, to a repayment out of the tax already received by the Exchequer, so that a large part of the sum received by the Government and spent during the war had to be repaid after the war. In this way the scheme had the final effect of a long-term loan to the Government, without interest, on very complicated lines. Inasmuch as taxpayers were forced to advance as duty to the Government during the war sums which they were afterwards entitled to take back as profits, it lost its character as pure taxation and took on the aspect of a repayable advance. But this forced loan had a distinct advantage to industry, inasmuch as concerns were compelled, on the fictitious or apparent prosperity of a rise in price, to hand over the proceeds, and many of them in 1920 were saved from the bankruptcy that might have followed the fall in prices.

The Post-war Fall in Prices

It is very interesting to read the anticipations of the results of a collapse in price long before the end of the war, and the proceedings of the Special Committee that sat to consider how it should be handled from the point of view of taxation. The mistake that people really made was to expect the collapse to come rather soon ; it was so long delayed that people thought it was not coming at all. When it did come, however, it bore out the worst fears of the most pessimistic. I well remember the sensation caused during the war by a phrase in a speech by Mr. Edwin Montagu, when he said that the State must ask her citizens to give up in taxes or loans half their income. This brought home the taxation burden of war more than any other single incident, and it was placarded in every street. In many instances, when the 80 per cent. tax was imposed and there was an income tax and super-tax of over 10s. in the £ on the balance of 20 per cent. remaining, the tax on the total excess, and sometimes on the total income, was over 90 per cent. At the end of the war taxation and inflation between them had made pretty fair havoc of steady-going business. There is probably some truth in the common contention that the Excess Profits Duty itself helped to keep up prices and to create inflation. Fortunes had been so seriously disturbed that it is no wonder that those who had been on the lucky side should still be the object of jealous attentions on the part of tax gatherers looking for sources of revenue. There was, therefore, a demand for an immediate attack on swollen fortunes, whether swollen by output or price or inflation, in order to adjust the national burdens of debt.

After-war Taxation

Soon after the war there was a great clamour for attacks upon *increase* of capital wealth made during the war. It was proposed to compare everyone's fortune at a particular date after the war with what they had before the war, and

to make a substantial levy upon the difference.
Some wanted a single or flat rate whatever the
margin or excess, and others wanted a progressive rate according to the amount of the excess.
The rival scheme was for a capital levy, and the
proposal for this had been under consideration
for some time. When it was first put forward,
especially by the economists, it was treated as
a kind of single composition for future taxes.
People said, " Why not take a lump of your
fortune at once, pay off debt with it, and so
lessen the interest charge on debt in future, and
therefore reduce your income tax for the future
—they were to be invited, that is to say, to pay
a lump sum forthwith in order to have lighter
taxes later on. But the arguments soon passed
from this stage. People talked about " conscrip-
tion of wealth "—" why should men be compelled to go into the trenches to be shot unless
there was some equal compulsion for those who
were allowed to stay at home to expose their
wealth to the risks of war?" This again passed into
a third type of argument, which said that a great
part of the debt had been incurred when prices
were very high ; it would have to be repaid
when prices were very low. People who had lent
to the State the equivalent of one pair of boots
would, in years to come, be receiving back the
equivalent of two if they were repaid the same
amount of money. What was the effect of these
two proposals ? The capital levy was deemed to
be in some respects more difficult than a levy on

war wealth, because the niceties and problems of capital valuation for the basis of a heavy duty might in themselves seriously affect the amount of tax payable, whereas war wealth was the *difference* between two valuations, and if the same kind of error took place in each valuation, the difference was unaffected. At the same time the war wealth proposal involved the work of two valuations ; one of them after a long period of time was " wisdom after the event," which is never a very good thing in valuations, whereas the capital levy demanded only one valuation. But the capital levy was inferior in one important respect of equity. A man might have had his fortune reduced owing to war losses from £100,000 to £50,000, and therefore be exceedingly unlucky. Another might have had his increased by war fortune from £10,000 to £50,000, and be exceedingly lucky. The duty payable in the two cases would be the same.

The levy on war wealth seemed, however, to fit the punishment according to the crime, or the burden to the fortune.

Towards the end of the inflationary period, when prices were still rising, that is, in the spring of 1920, it was desired to make an heroic effort to pay off some of the dangerous short-term or " floating debt," and a Special Committee sat to consider this taxing of war wealth. Before, however, its findings could be given any practical effect the storm had burst and prices had begun to collapse, valuation became more and more difficult and changeable, fortunes were reduced, and the danger in a special tax of this kind of creating a collapse of commercial credit became greater. That, then, was the last we heard of this particular impost, but the agitation for the capital levy went on, though its difficulties on a falling price level became more and more obvious. It was seen that a valuation at the end of 1919, say in the case of ships, would become in eighteen months or two years, without any change of assets, less than the actual amount of duty assessed, and inasmuch as provision was necessary for payment by instalments, this would have led to absolute chaos. It is impossible to have any large-scale taxation based upon valuations in times of rapidly changing prices, because these changes not only falsify the valuations after they are made, but as taxation takes time to collect, they completely alter the whole relation between the amount to be paid and the basis of assessment from what was intended.

The Labour Government of 1924 appointed a Committee, known as the Colwyn Committee, to report, amongst other matters, on the capital levy, and their Report, which took some years to publish, was adverse to it. It was shown that the effect of a levy, the greater part of the yield of which must come from the larger fortunes, was to deplete the fortunes chargeable later on to death duties and income tax to a very important extent. In other words, the State could not take its bite three times, or hardly even twice. The second and third bites were bound to be correspondingly smaller. When the whole matter was weighed up over a period of years, there was far less in this financially for the Exchequer than appeared at first sight. At the same time, we are bound to see that if a levy could have been imposed when prices were at their highest, if it could have been valued and collected quickly before prices fell, and if it could have been applied to the repayment of debt, without causing a collapse of credit—if these several things could have been done, then it would have been an excellent thing to pay off debt while prices were high, and thus save the increasing burden as prices fell. But the technical difficulties were too great, and time was of the essence of the contract, while the movement of prices was exceedingly rapid.

The After-war Task

What in a word or two was the task before us after the war ? The war itself created a new attitude towards what the State could afford for social services—in pensions, health insurance, education and the like. But apart altogether from the social burdens, the sum due for debt and pensions was equal to twice the old budget alone, and the country had to face an 800 million £ budget (four times the old figure), the major part of which was unalterable, *whatever the price level*. As prices fall and the same activities of the country are measured in different values, the total national income in money goes down, but this charge for the debt stands. Four hundred million £ for debt is only one-tenth of a national income of 4,000 million £, but when prices have fallen 20 per cent., and this income becomes, say, 3,200 million £ (assuming no actual increase in the real goods and services on the heap), then the 400 million £ annual debt charge becomes one-eighth. Thus the same amount of taxation is an increasing burden after deflation.

Some Comparisons

Let us look at one or two of the facts. Internal debt in 1818 after the Napoleonic War took 8·12 per cent., or with pensions, 9·42 per cent. of income. Immediately before the Great War this had sunk to 1·07 per cent. for the internal debt, or 1·61 per cent. to include all kinds of pensions. By 1923, when war finance had settled down into its routine, internal and external debt requirements amounted to 9·13 per cent., pensions, etc., 2·45 per cent., or a total of 11·58 per cent. The ratio of the *total tax revenue* to the national income was just over 14 per cent. in 1818, but it was practically 19 per cent. in 1923. There was, however, a very different distribution of this burden at the two periods. After the Napoleonic Wars debts and taxation, on the whole, were more burdensome or more oppressive to the poorer classes. The burden per head became less during the century, owing to the rapid increase in population and the remarkable Victorian burst of industrial progress. Thus if we reckon

the income per head as 100 in 1818, and the debt
charge per head also 100, before 1875 the income
per head was 257, but the debt charge only 72,
and by 1913 the income per head was 400, but
the debt charge only 52, or one-eighth as heavy.

The extent to which taxation is burdensome
after war depends, then, on three things. First, the
rate of increase of the population ; secondly, the
expansion of industry and science ; and thirdly,
the level of prices. Now, we cannot expect to get
the relief through an *increase* of population that
was afforded in the last century, for the rate of
natural increase was very great then and is
very small now. There is no sign that industry
will expand on anything like the same scale, but
against this we must remember that no real
prosperity came to England for twenty years
after the Napoleonic Wars. There were long
periods of very great difficulty, singularly
parallel point by point to recent years, and it
was not until the middle of the century that the
real advance took place. When it did come it
was coincident, not merely with scientific
expansion, but also with the " warming up " of
the price level due to the new discoveries of gold
in California and Australia.

We can look at the total burden of taxation
during war by comparing the percentages due
from different types of income before and after.
The taxation percentage on an income of £100
before the Great War was 5·4, and after 14·1 ;
on an income of £500 it was 4·4 and became 8 ;

and on an income of £5,000 before the war it ranged from 6·7 to 9·6, whereas afterwards this became 28·5 to 32·6 per cent. (the variation being according to the extent to which the income was derived from personal exertion or from investment). In the case of incomes of £50,000 a year the rate of tax before the war ranged from 8·4 to 13·6, and after the war from 48 to 60 per cent. There was no question that foreigners were universally impressed by the effort made in this country to pay for the war by taxation. We raised the amount produced by taxation from 200 million £ in a year to 1,000 million £. In the six years from 1914 to 1920 there was a total expenditure of 11,268 million £. Of this 3,605 million £ was produced by tax revenue, 466 million £ by sale of war property, or a percentage of 36·13, and 7,196 million £ were borrowed, or a percentage of 63·87. Our taxation revenue (without the Post Office) went in the following order for the six years: 189, 290, 514 (including 140 Excess Profits Duty), 613, 784, 999 = 3,389 (millions of £). The percentages corresponding were: 35, 22, 26, 26, 34·5, 80·56 = 36·13, as shown above.

It has been pointed out by one well-known American authority that our expenditure in six years exceeded the aggregate of our expenditure in the previous 226 years, which included eight major wars. A rough calculation of the burden to be borne compared with the national wealth shows that after the French wars one hundred years ago, the percentage of debt to wealth was

31·48 ; after the Boer War it was 6·13 ; before the Great War it was 4·87, and after the Great War 33·65. The annual charge as a burden upon annual income was 8 per cent. after the Napoleonic Wars ; 1·6 after the Boer War ; 1·06 before the Great War, and 10 per cent. afterwards. How much of the cost was met from taxation ? Some 63 per cent. of the Napoleonic Wars ; 38·6 of the Boer War, and from 28·74 to 36·13 for the World War (according to the way in which the realisation of war property is dealt with). The expenditure per head was £4 4s. for the French War, £4·15 for the Boer War, £4·7 before the Great War, and £35 14s. as at December 1919. What percentages did the different countries bear in taxation, excluding loans from their expenditure ? Up to March 1919 in the case of Great Britain 30·1, France 17, Italy 14·7, Germany 11·7. The United States, of course, did not come in until 1917, after which their percentage was 36.

In France the situation was very different. It has been well said :

It is clear, then, that the outbreak of the war found France financially unprepared. Her revenue system, with its highly elaborated indirect taxes and its entirely antiquated direct taxes, was inadequate to meet even the relatively insignificant pre-war demands. When war was declared, England had immediately available a well-seasoned income tax and supertax, administered by an admirable civil service. When the need came, it was necessary only to increase rates.

Superficially the French figures look heroic, but the effect of inflation has to be allowed for.

The following figures show the amount of the French tax collections before the war and afterwards :

FRENCH TAX COLLECTIONS

					Paper Francs.	Real Values (Billions).
1913	.	.	.	.	4·1	4·1
1919	.	.	.	.	10·0	2·8
1920	.	.	.	.	18·3	3·6
1923	.	.	.	.	20·9	5·0
1926	.	.	.	.	38·1	5·4
1927	.	.	.	.	43·7	7·0

The first column shows the amount paid in paper francs, which were of course reduced in value, and the second column the collection reduced to pre-war gold equivalence. The average annual tax collections for the whole war and post-war period were 4·15 billion francs, or almost the same as the 4·07 billion collected during 1913, so that very little indeed has been contributed to the costs of war or reconstruction. Of course in the last two or three years since the effort to stabilise the franc the situation has changed materially. We are concerned here with the aftermath of war, and the comments of an authoritative American economist are of particular importance :

In terms of pre-war francs the 1918 collections were only about half as great as the 1913 collections. During the five years 1914–18, the French spent approximately five borrowed francs for every franc from revenue receipts. The revenues in 1914, although not half large enough to meet the total expenditures, did nevertheless suffice to meet the total cost of the civil service, the total debt service and a small part of the military expenses. In 1915 they were insufficient to meet even civil service and debt charges. By 1918 the civil services alone demanded more than the total collections.

Haig has said that the taxation policy was unforgivably weak and vacillating.

According to the analysis generally accepted, the French, confronted with a great financial problem, showed an incapacity to tax themselves with the courage and resourcefulness displayed by the English and Americans. . . . As a foreigner gains a familiarity with the background of French public finance, as he reads the public documents of the period and studies the character of the financial problem as it presented itself from time to time to the successive ministers of finance, he finds himself questioning the correctness of the current diagnosis and the justice of the unqualified condemnation so commonly meted out to France. . . . Thus the French have scarcely begun to develop the conception of the State as a convenient device for accomplishing specific ends approved by a democratic people, fully aware of the costs involved and willing and eager to pay the bills. In this respect the French are backward. . . . " When I consider the French tax system," remarked one ancient senator to the writer, " I am impressed with the truth of the Italian saying : ' One walks easily in an old shoe.' " That an old tax is a painless tax seems to have been generally accepted as true almost without limitations. A new tax, simply because of its newness, was under a great initial handicap. When the war broke out France had only old shoes in her wardrobe.

The aftermath of war in taxation is worse now for this country than for any other, and than for any previous war. It is true that the advance of a policy of social expenditure might have come about without any war, and modern budgets might in any case have been much larger than

of old. But the war did two great things : First
it gave rise to pressing social emergencies, such
as widespread unemployment and the housing
problem, with a rigid level of wage costs ; and
secondly, it proved what an immense fund of
annual wealth available for redistribution by
taxation could be tapped by high rates of income
tax, supertax and death duties, without immediate disaster, even if at the consequence
of ultimate decline.

II

I have explained already that in utilising the heap of production for war purposes, after the State has done all that it can to induce the people that remain behind to maintain the heap or increase it as far as possible, there are three ways in which the State can secure the share it wants.

Let us assume that the heap is maintained in size, and that every item on it is represented by a purchasing ticket. The Government can take over a ticket and use it instead of the individual doing so, either finally, which is taxation, or under a promise that out of the heaps of future years the State will then secure a compulsory title by taxation and hand the equivalent tickets over to the original lender or his heirs. But the Government can also leave the individuals in possession of their tickets, and privily make a lot more. If the storekeeper in charge of the heap continues to give out one unit of production for each ticket, he will soon find that the Government tickets have helped to clear out the whole of the heap and there will be many tickets over. If there are two vouchers in existence for every one there was before and no increase in the goods to be given out, the storekeeper quickly finds that the produce per ticket is halved. In other words, prices have gone up to double. It is now necessary to hand in two tickets to get out a particular quantity of production. Thus a new level of exchange is set up between purchasing units and goods to be purchased. It is a very small matter what the number of units actually is; the thing that matters is the way that number is changed from time to time. In the year in question, when the Government has made its claim it has by this means come into possession of a considerable part of the heap. It is really a system of silent confiscatory taxation. The next year, assuming that the number of tickets remains in circulation amongst the people, for the storekeeper has given out all these tickets as the heap has been piled up, and the new level of exchange is two tickets for one unit, if the Government is going to get hold of part of the national heap in the same way (in addition to taxation and loans), it must repeat the process and make another lot of tickets or notes, and so prices go up again.

The Attraction of Inflation

Why do governments almost invariably, in wartime and afterwards, have to resort to this expedient? First, because most people have to be kept reasonably sweet-tempered, sometimes even the most patriotic, to go on producing hard, and because taxation is psychologically repressive in production. The lessened reward and the smaller fund for reinvestment in new capital have their aggregate effect. Secondly, because loans also have a definite limit—a limit of credit (in the State) and personal inclination (in the lender). But inflation of the currency is easy, and more or less unsuspected and unnoticed while it is going on. If skilfully done, prices creep up, and real rewards in wages and interest are reduced slowly, while business enterprise and employment receive a great fillip.

Let us define inflation therefore as an increase of vouchers or purchasing power compared with commodities. There are other factors involved, which the economists call " velocity," relating to the rapidity with which vouchers are turned over and used again and again, but that need not bother us here. I will ask four questions :

(1) Did it happen ?

(2) How did it happen ?

(3) Why did it happen ?

(4) What were its effects ?

Did Inflation Occur ?

First of all to see whether it happened. Let us look at the British figures, and start with a price level of 100 in 1913. What is meant by a *price level* ? It is intended to describe the " general purchasing power of money." Let us suppose we set out a miscellaneous stock of goods of all kinds, so that nearly every kind of production is represented, and that the quantity so set out or scheduled can be bought for £100. If next year, to obtain the same parcel or schedule, we have to pay £200, you say the " price level has risen," in fact " doubled." If it can be bought for £50, you say the " price level has fallen," or money has become more valuable, whichever way you like to put it. This does not mean that the prices of the *individual articles* in the parcel have all changed in this way—some may have gone up and some gone down, but it is the general effect over the whole that we refer to as " the price level."

Now, here are the figures. The first column shows the price level, starting with £100 :

					Total Circulation of Notes and Deposits.
1913	.	.	.	. 100	100
1915	.	.	.	. 138	126
1917	.	.	.	. 228	174
1918	.	.	.	. 232	222
1919 December	.	.	. 280	245

By April 1920 the price level had risen to 325, but in twenty months, by December 1921, it was down to a half of this figure. I think you will see clearly from these figures that *inflation had happened*, and that there was a rough correspondence between the total purchasing power and the price level. For the second column is an indication of the total number of vouchers or tickets in the hands of the producers of the heap. Paper money at the beginning of the war was quite new to us, except for £5 notes in England and

£1 notes in Scotland. In times of stress other
countries do not trust each other's paper money
—it is too easy to manufacture paper money, and
paper money is only a promise to pay—what ?—
whatever it will fetch ! But they do trust solid
gold, and so in order to keep our gold resources
where they were of the greatest use and advantage, we replaced gold in the people's pockets
with paper, by the issue at the outbreak of war
of £1 and 10s. notes. Do not imagine that the
use of paper money is necessarily " inflation "—
far from it. If *instead* of sovereigns or half-
sovereigns you have £1 and 10s. notes, there is no
inflation in that. My younger listeners will hardly
realise what a revolution it was for many people
to handle flimsy pieces of paper and to regard
them as valuable. At the outbreak of war it was
my job at the Inland Revenue—for these new
notes were Government notes—to deal with the
many claims for spoilt notes. Many people, particularly the older ones and the poorer ones, did
the most fantastic things with their notes, and
then discovered afterwards what had happened !
They were wrapped round the cheese and eaten
by the mice ! They were often used as pipe
lighters inadvertently ! There was no accident
too wild or improbable during the first few
months of the note issue. We had to devise
rough-and-ready tests for the reimbursement of
these losses, which would protect the poor users
from their own blunders while at the same
time protecting the Exchequer against fraud.

Whether notes were inadvertently torn into little bits in envelopes that people thought were empty, or carried about in pockets until they were worn to threads, or burnt, or reduced to pulp by liquids, my task was a heavy one. But this by the way !

As soon as the quantity of paper money gets out of ratio not merely to the gold it replaces, but also to the goods that it has to buy and that are being currently produced, then inflation sets in. It must not be supposed that inflation occurs only in the fighting countries. The truth of what is called the " quantity theory"—that is, the economic principle which connects prices with the number of tickets as compared with the goods on the national heap—is shown by illustrations from other countries. In Switzerland before the war the total purchasing media came to 454 million francs, and in 1922 it was about 920, say double. The level of prices rose one and two-thirds. In Norway the expansion of currency was 2·7 and of prices 2·3. In Finland the increase in currency was tenfold, and prices rose eleven times. There are influences at work which keep the proportions from being exact, but this is a sufficiently close correspondence.[1]

How Inflation Takes Place

My second question is, " How does it happen ? " The most obvious way is, of course, by direct Government issues of notes. When Governments

[1] Lehfeldt, *Money*, p. 97.

wish to buy goods that have been made, and
they have no more funds by taxation and
borrowing, if they are in charge of the note issue
they can print whatever they want and go into
the market with them. But the more usual way,
and the way in this country, was by borrowing
from the central bank by what we should call
" Ways and Means " advances. Let me give
you a classic description of what this means.
Lord Cunliffe's Committee on Currency and
Foreign Exchanges after the war put it as
follows :

The powers given to the Government by Parliament to
borrow from the Bank of England in the form of an overdraft on the credit of Ways and Means were, as the name
implies, intended to enable the Government to anticipate
receipts from revenue or permanent borrowings for a brief
period only. Indeed, Parliament, by expressly providing
that all such advances should be repaid in the quarter
following that in which they were obtained, showed that it
had no intention of bestowing upon the Government the
power of securing an overdraft of indefinite duration and
amount. Under the exigencies of war finance the Government found it necessary to re-borrow in each quarter on the
credit of Ways and Means the amount needed to enable them
to comply with the statutory requirement that the previous
quarter's Ways and Means Advances should be repaid, with
the result that the total outstanding advances remained for
a long time at a high figure. . . . This process has had
results of such far-reaching importance that it may be
useful to set out in detail the manner in which it operates.
Suppose, for example, that in a given week the Government
require £10,000,000 over and above the receipts from taxation and loans from the public. They apply for an advance
from the Bank of England, which by a book entry places

the amount required to the credit of Public Deposits in the same way as any other banker credits the account of a customer when he grants him temporary accommodation. The amount is then paid out to contractors and other Government creditors, and passes, when the cheques are cleared, to the credit of their bankers in the books of the Bank of England—in other words, is transferred from " Public " to " Other " deposits, the effect of the whole transaction thus being to increase by £10,000,000 the purchasing power in the hands of the public in the form of deposits in the joint-stock banks and the bankers' cash at the Bank of England by the same amount. The bankers' liabilities to depositors having thus increased by £10,000,000 and their cash reserves by an equal amount, their proportion of cash to liabilities (which was normally before the war something under 20 per cent.) is improved, with the result that they are in a position to make advances to their customers to an amount equal to four or five times the sum added to their cash reserves, or, in the absence of demand for such accommodation, to increase their investments by the difference between the cash received and the proportion they require to hold against the increase of their deposit liabilities. Since the outbreak of war it is the second procedure which has in the main been followed, the surplus cash having been used to subscribe for Treasury Bills and other Government securities. The money so subscribed has again been spent by the Government and returned in the manner above described to the bankers' cash balances, the process being repeated again and again, until each £10,000,000 originally advanced by the Bank of England has created new deposits representing new purchasing power to several times that amount.

This, to a beginner, may be a little forbidding as an explanation, but is well worth study.

Let us look at what happened when a new war loan was issued and a strong patriotic appeal was made to subscribe. It was possible to raise the money by making things last longer. You can say, " I was going to buy, as usual, a new suit this spring, or a new frock for Easter Sunday, but, in spite of what people say, I will keep on with last year's, and apply the money instead to the new loan." Or you could do without some actual and usual expenditure. Your maid has left to go into a munition factory and, instead of employing another, you do the work yourself, and play less tennis and bridge. What would have been paid for her wages you could then apply to the new war loan. This is the direct method of subscription, and obviously involves no inflation, because you have gone without some goods or services on the heap, and handed over to the Government the right to take those goods or services, either going without them entirely yourself, or replacing them by making them for yourself.

But there was a second method of subscription, which was much encouraged, and which gave rise to inflation. If you were not prepared to wear last year's suit or frock, or to go without any household services, you might go to the bank and say, " I want to take up a thousand pounds of the new war loan—will you advance me £950 to do it ? " Obviously, nobody *at this stage* has given up any title to withdraw what is on the heap. You are maintaining your claim upon it as usual, and yet the Government are somehow mysteriously getting a thousand pounds too— that must give rise to inflation. There is all the difference in the world between transferring your right to certain goods and handing over rights without giving up your own. When once your £1,000 in rights had been handed over to the Government, they then "pulverised" their purchasing power into little lots in notes which went into circulation. Very largely these notes got into circulation through payments of wages to workers on Government work. These wage earners were producing articles that went abroad for the war, but the wages they got they spent on home production, food, etc., the very things that you were also spending your income on. If you had given up nothing, then by this bank loan you had enabled these wage earners to compete with *their* new vouchers with your original or actual vouchers, and—up went the prices !

Was Inflation Necessary ?

My third question is, " Why did it happen ? " No doubt you incline to feel very superior, and to say that inflation is a terribly bad thing, that an honest Government ought not to do it, and so on and so forth ! But you should not blame too much. War is urgent, compelling beyond all human imagining; and even after the war the burdens of the State are real. Inflation creeps in by a hundred ways ; it is an immediate remedy ; it often requires no permission, no Acts of Parliament ; and the psychology of the governed and the Government all lead direct into inflationary paths. But, as we have seen, having once got on to a scale of expenditure through inflation, it has to be repeated after a time to secure the same results. You are helpless to stop yourself ; it is like running downhill—beyond a point you either go faster and faster, or fall over ! It is easy enough to *say* that inasmuch as a war can only be fought by current production, it should all be done by taxation alone—it is quite another thing to *do* it. In a perfect world, with perfect economic understanding and perfect patriotism, no doubt it could be done, but then in a perfect world there would be no war.

The Results of Inflation

My fourth question is, " What are the effects ? " You have seen how the Government can get hold of more of the heap by inflation, and how the price level is rapidly raised thereby. Unfortunately, however, the individual claims to the heap are not all affected alike or evenly ; there is much disparity—some are ruined and some are enriched. For this alteration in the price level changes the proportions of what is due to the different parties in all that is left. While inflation is going on it robs everyone who is entitled to fixed money payments or a fixed number of tickets, i.e. everyone who has lent £100 at one date finds when he gets it back that he can take far less off the heap than he sacrificed originally.

The business man who is continually receiving
more and more tickets for his products in the
new and rising prices finds that he has to pay
out only the same number as he did before for
rent, and for debenture interest, and for other
payments, including wages. For a given volume
of sales, for which he previously received a
thousand tickets of purchasing power, he now,
we will say, if prices have been doubled, receives
two thousand, but he has to pay away in wages,
say, five hundred and in interest another two
hundred, making seven hundred in all. He
formerly had three hundred, and now he has
thirteen hundred tickets left for himself. He gets
a proportion of the total number of tickets
received, which was formerly three-tenths, and
is now six and a half tenths, whereas the former
recipients of the rent and the debenture interest
get the same number of tickets, and find that
they will buy only half as much. This sounds
very crude, and the business man while it is
happening is very rarely actually aware of what
is going on. He finds business is good and
profits are rising ; he is tempted to expand his
business and increase his trade.

Making money while inflation is going on
is as easy as falling off a log, and yet the
average man thinks to himself what a fine
fellow he is. He gets a great feeling of prosperity, and there is general optimism in all
directions. Even the banks are affected ; they
see that business is brisk, sales are good, and

therefore they are ready to extend credit, all of which means an addition to the inflationary element. Money is so easily made that it soon leads to speculation, and to the putting forward of business schemes that in times of purely stable prices would not offer very much attraction. For a time the wage earner is not aware of what is happening. Perhaps he first of all becomes envious of the large profits that are being made, and thinks that he should get a share in the increased prosperity. In fact, the goods that the business man is able to buy with his income may not be more numerous than they used to be, but we are so unconscious of money inflation that increased dividends and increased profits are looked upon as increases in themselves, apart altogether from any increased purchasing power they may possess. But the wage earner subsequently discovers that the " cost of living " is rising and that his wages do not go so far as they did. He then puts in an application for an increase of money wage. These rises in wages generally lag behind the rises in prices, and good profits continue to be made. But all this time the very movement of inflation is sowing the seeds of its own nemesis. In the first place, schemes that are not in themselves really sound, or only sound in boom conditions, tend to be too easily undertaken. In the second, each business man estimates for himself, and without the knowledge of the others, and thinks that he is going to get a good share of the increased market, so that ultimately the aggregate expansion on the part of all the business men is far too great for any reasonable demand at the prices they had individually considered possible. If each business man increases his output 50 per cent. on the understanding that the price will remain where it is, then with what we call " elasticity of demand," it means that if the supply is very great, it can only be taken off at much reduced prices. This very factor is his undoing, because there is a glut of his particular commodity. Then again, a good deal of the profit that is made is not spent in consumption goods which have been produced so freely, but is saved and put in the bank for investment and production goods, new factories, etc. Then the position arises that the market required for consumption goods is much extended by the new machinery and the new factories for which this saving is provided, and it is seen that that market is becoming doubtful and limited. At that point the outlook undergoes a change. When the change comes, of course there is a tendency to anticipate the fall, and all the new capitalisation of businesses becomes a wrong one—wages in the calculation may perhaps be too high for the new receipts of the business man—too large a proportion of what he gets, and they are at once much more difficult to adjust downwards, particularly since the cost of living does not fall as rapidly as wholesale prices.

The whole process of inflation has led to wild

extravagance and lack of proportion between different types of expenditure. Renewed confidence for additional speculation, to keep up the balloon, so to speak, can only be obtained by increasing the instalment of inflation. When it stops it has just the same effect upon business as when you tread upon the top step in the dark that isn't there! But there is an even more potent influence in keeping inflation on a steady crescendo. While it is going on it has a very important effect on the national budget. Many of the Government's expenses for materials and purchases of all kinds feel the full brunt of the increased prices. They should receive, of course, increased taxes, such as those upon profits in income tax, but here there is nearly always a lag before the profits of a particular year have their effect upon the budget—the year has to be completed, the accounts have to be made up, the liabilities computed with reference to the revenue, and then the demands have to be sent out, and by the time the taxpayer is ready to hand over the money, it represents what was due on a basis long before. If profits and prices have been rising in the meantime, it is obvious that the amount to be received will not represent the circumstances of the day when it is paid, but of some time before. In the income tax, when it was upon a three-year average, the years 1, 2 and 3 became the basis for the year 4, and the tax was paid in the year 5.

During the inflation period in Germany, the lag

in the real value of the mark paid to the Government compared with the amount the Government was paying out at the same time was very extraordinary, and was the main cause of the deficiency in the budget which led to currency manufacture and chaos. In the Dawes Report we stated, " Although the rates of income tax according to the nominal scales rose to nearly 60 per cent. on the highest incomes, statistics of cases furnished to us by the German Government show that in effect the burden of actual tax, measured in gold, on the higher incomes, instead of being 50 to 60 per cent. was only half those rates upon the income of the year (measured in gold)." When the deficit is rising through inflation, it nearly always means that the easiest way to balance the budget is to make still more currency—more than business itself would have asked for. This in turn creates another deficit the following year, and more notes have to be printed by the Government to secure what it needs from the national heap. Even customs duties do not rise to the occasion, so to speak, when prices are going up. What we call *ad valorem* duties, i.e. a percentage of the total price or value, will of course result in handing over to the Government an increased number of units and tickets according to the increased purchasing price. But specific duties (e.g. so many shillings per ton), when the price per ton has very greatly increased, obviously represent a much smaller percentage of the total value. If the

Government have to buy any of these tons at the enhanced price, they will indeed find that their receipts for taxation have shrunk in relation to their total expenses.

The experts reporting upon the results of inflation in France in 1926 said :

At a time of monetary depreciation, however much care one may take to speed up collections, the gold value of the tax gradually shrinks between the times of assessment and collection. Repressions and increases in rates may well be applied, but they only encourage the export of capital and accentuate, indirectly, the exchange crisis. . . . The history of the customs since 1914 is one of intricate and almost constant change. The import prohibitions and export restrictions of war-times were followed by a system of ever-rising coefficients applied to the normal tariff duties, in an effort to keep the rates up to the advancing price level.

Professor Haig gives these reasons for the failure of the customs revenue in France to grow :

(1) Almost all the duties are specific, and though individual rates were increased by administrative decrees after the war, and though the Chamber later raised them 30 per cent. at a time, twice they appear never to have caught up with the rising price level ; (2) the duties are protective—revenue is not their sole, or even their chief aim. Much of the heavy imports of raw materials which France works up in her factories enters duty-free.

There is a third way in which inflation once started tends to lead on and on, and it lies in the effect upon the rates of exchange. If foreigners, or indeed even the residents of a country, get a notion that a country's money is going to be worth less and less in its purchasing power, then they will try to hold as little of that money as possible, and if they have any of it on hand they will try to sell it for other currencies, which means a " flight from the mark," or from the franc or from sterling. It may be something brought about from purely psychological causes, mainly fear or excessive caution—a desire to hold one's wealth in some other form than the currency of a particular country. This leads to diminished purchasing power of the currency in foreign trade, and more and more marks, or francs, or whatever it may be, having to be produced in order to exchange for the requisite amount of foreign currency to buy goods abroad.

Inflation in Germany

These three ways, then—the psychology of business, desiring to stave off the day when lack of confidence will ensue ; the desire of the Government to make up the lag in its budget ; and the foreign exchange difficulty—these three ways are most important in working up inflation to a position of great difficulty. The most striking perhaps of all cases were those of Germany and Russia. I will not bother about Russia because her industries are so unsettled and her political scheme so different, but Germany is a country like our own, industrialised and with a strong banking system, and therefore a good example for us to take for " the aftermath of war." Now, during the war the rise in prices in Germany was not so very great ; it was, say,

from 1 to 2½ by 1918. It was after the war that
the trouble began. It became 8 times by the
end of 1919, and 17 times by March 1920.
This became critical for other people besides
themselves, because finance is interwoven
between different nations, and this kind of thing
cannot happen on such a scale without affecting
those abroad who have wealth in such a country.
But after March 1920 the Germans got their
inflation situation a bit in hand, just as everybody else did, and prices fell—the price level
was only 14 times the pre-war figure in August
1921. Then some important political events happened. The pressure of reparation payments on
a country which was depleted of its circulating
capital began to be severe, so it had risen again
to 34 by the end of 1921. Then there was a
twentyfold depreciation in four months, and by
July 1922 the price level was 100 times the pre-
war level, in October 556, and in December 1922,
1,425 times. Then came Germany's chief difficulties and the occupation of the Ruhr, and by
June 1923 the price level had risen to 19,000
times pre-war, July 74,000, August 944,000.
Then began the astronomical climb—24 million
times the next month, 7,000 odd millions in
October ; 725,000 millions in November, and
1,261,000 millions in December was the multiplier that had to be used. This old currency had
become perfectly impossible to use, ridiculous in
its daily movements, and a new currency had to
be invented. A currency called the rentenmark,

which I will not describe in detail, was substituted, and of course it had to be given some
equivalent in prices of the old currency. The old
currency was represented by 1 with twelve
noughts after it—one million million—that
equalled one of the new rentenmarks. All these
deceptive issues of notes, and alterations of the
denominations on the existing notes, had made
the *foreign* value of the currency less in kind,
even in total, so that—so far from inflation keeping up the total purchasing power of the mark—
its aggregate purchasing power became less and
less. This is when inflation gets into its third
stage, and is completely ineffective to achieve
its object.

Now let us look at the social effects in Germany.
Of course those who had debts, in the way of
mortgages and debentures of a fixed money
value, were able to wipe them out with hardly
any expense at all. An indebtedness of 100,000
marks when the total value of a property is
200,000 is 50 per cent., but when the total value
of the property is fifty times as great—for, when
I say value, I mean " price " in the new notes—
then this debt is only a fiftieth part of itself, in
fact, only 1 per cent. So old debts in money, and
pensions and the like, all became negligible—
wiped out ! The old National Debt became
absolutely unimportant. This particular situation is not, however, what makes the German
of to-day go into a cold perspiration at the
thought of having any repetition of the inflation

Social conditions and problems of Inflations: Price Level.

of those days. No, it is rather the social effects amongst those who are handling money in the form of wages and retail purchases day by day. The wage rate had to be altered by a multiplier at the most frequent intervals. The wage earner stood in queues and the moment he received his wage it was snatched from him by a member of his family, who would rush off to the shops in order to turn it into goods before the prices in the shops were altered. They were sometimes altered at intervals two or three times in a day, and the shops were shut while the goods were repriced. Inasmuch as in a few minutes the purchasing power of a given wage could be halved, here was an experience that will never be forgotten. It was a nightmare that has sunk deep into the German national thought.[1] The Dawes Committee was sitting when the full effect of it was still present in everybody's mind, and in Berlin the representatives of labour appeared before us, and one question was put to them : " What can this Committee do for German labour ? " They did not ask for one of the slogans of labour, such as the eight-hour day,

[1] " Everyone who was unfortunate enough to possess mark currency was in danger of having it lose half its value in his pocket overnight, and the moment people received payments in marks they dashed off with the money to buy food, clothes, houses, scrap iron, or anything else which had an inherent worth, and which would not waste away. In addition the more fortunate ones bought foreign exchange, and thus got their funds out of the country. Indeed, later on the depreciation became so rapid that prices in many shops were adjusted to the exchange rates every hour or two, and eventually were fixed outright in foreign currencies."—*The Recovery of Germany*, James W. Angell.

old age or disability pensions, or insurance
against unemployment, or any kind of social
expenditure. Their answer came promptly,
" What you can do for German labour is to give
us a stable currency." " Do you know," the
representatives of German labour said, " that
for many months it has been impossible for a
wage earner in Germany to perform any of his
moral obligations, knowing that a child was
coming to the family at a certain time, there was
no way by which the husband through effort, or
sacrifice, or saving, could guarantee his wife a
doctor and a nurse when that event arrived."
One, knowing that his mother was stricken with
a fatal disease, could not by any extra effort or
sacrifice, or saving, be in a position to ensure her
a decent burial on her death. So you cannot
wonder that they wanted, just as a basic human
thing, a stable currency, assuring the worker
that his wages would have the same purchasing
power when he wanted to spend them as when he
earned them.[1] It was even said that it cost more
money to pay for a ride in a taxi-cab than a taxi-
cab would hold.

An American professor, Dr. Angell, gives a
well-balanced summary of the effects in Germany :

The group which suffered most from the inflation, however,
was the group which was also least able to defend itself: the
middle classes among the town dwellers. The industrialists
and agriculturists had on the whole little to complain of,

[1] *Vide* my *Criticism and other Addresses*, p. 73.

and labour had always the last resort of the strike, but the middle classes had nothing. Composed largely of people with small fixed incomes, such as salaried officials and clerks, recipients of pensions and little investors living on interest and rent—of whom the latter group were hit especially hard by the Government control of city rentals—they were precisely the group most exposed to the evil consequences of currency depreciation, while they lacked both the knowledge and the opportunity to combat it. Their savings disappeared, their pensions and annuities melted away, and the sons who might have supported them had all too commonly been killed in the war. Hundreds of thousands of educated men and women, too old or feeble or untrained to earn their own living, were abruptly faced with starvation. Many died. The others, passing from day to day without hope, survived only by the sacrifice of treasured books, furniture, jewellery and all their saleable possessions, and at the end by domestic and foreign charity. Their history is one of the most genuinely pitiful chapters in all the war and post-war tragedy. Such were the principal changes in the distribution of wealth and income which the inflation brought about. The net effect was to increase enormously the share of the industrialists and agriculturists, at the expense of the workers and the middle classes. The gain arose chiefly from the wiping out of the old industrial mortgages and debentures, which had been extensively held by the small investors ; and from the forced sale, in return for worthless currency, of a great deal of other securities, land and property, which were directly or indirectly bought by the people who hold financial power to-day. In addition, the wiping out of most of the old debt of the Reich and the other governments, likewise held primarily by small investors, has made the burden of taxation which industry and finance must bear distinctly smaller than it would otherwise have been ; and has thus in effect operated to transfer a further quantity of wealth and income from the middle classes to the financial and industrial leaders.[1]

---

[1] *The Recovery of Germany.*

A similar picture for Russia was drawn by Mr. Keynes in graphic terms :

In Moscow unwillingness to hold money except for the shortest possible time reaches a fantastic intensity. If you buy a pound of cheese in a grocer's shop, the grocer runs off with the roubles as fast as his legs will carry him to the central market to replenish his stocks by changing them into cheese again, lest they lose their value before he gets there. This is what keeps the new bourgeoisie so thin, and justifies the prevision of economists in naming the phenomenon " velocity of circulation."

The Reasons for Inflation

What was the reason for inflation going to such terrible extremes ? First of all, taxation was not severe enough or prompt enough ; its collection by the newly formed central Government, with only a gradually asserted power over the local authorities, was not sufficiently strong. The position of State finance is very difficult for any-one who has not lived in Germany or studied the history of its development to understand fully. Prussia, Saxony, Bavaria and other States each have a very large amount of authority that has worked and still works havoc with anything like a central control of the financial position, and foreigners have complained that the parishes or communes are insufficiently controlled by the State in the matter of expenditure. Some blame attaches also to the industrialists. They confused their own swollen profits with prosperity, and had too little regard for the ultimate results of their action. The royal road to success was through borrowed money, and when the sums

borrowed had depreciated in the following year
and could be easily repaid in depreciated marks
it lead to high profits.[1]

Inflation in France

The story of the French paper money of the
Revolution has often been told. It was the
classic example of the spectacular effect of
almost unlimited issues of paper money until the
Great War. They introduced them with their
eyes open. Dupont de Nemours reminded them
of the recent experience of the United States
"which ten years before had issued notes guaran-
teed by the Government, with its immense
resources, its men of trusted probity like
Washington and Franklin, and yet had come to
such a pass that a pair of boots fetched 36,000
livres of paper money, and a supper for four
persons, at an ordinary cash price of 10 dollars,
cost 50,000 livres in paper."[2] At first the assignats
were very successful, but as the Treasury funds
became exhausted, recourse was had to issues
again and again. From the original issue of 400
million francs in 1790, they soon reached 3,750
millions, and they sank to one-fifth in value.
Futile attempts were made to control prices, but
the maximum prices produced no sales, as

---

[1] When these lectures were delivered, the actual consequences of
inflation were very little known to the young people of this country,
but of course, prior to the coming off the gold standard, and during
the budget emergency, the horrors of inflation were very luridly set
out by various speakers. There is no reason to suppose, if inflation
once got well away from monetary moorings, that we should fare
better than Germany or France. With our large foreign deposits, a
real flight from the pound might have very spectacular results.

[2] *Cambridge Modern History*, vol. viii.

depreciation continued, for by 1794 there were
8,000 million in issue. Trade was completely
paralysed. As wages were not advanced sufficiently rapidly, people refused to work. The
Directory had a great time as money makers, and
by 1796 there were 45,500 million, and they had
become practically valueless—in fact, the issues
stopped when it cost more to print them than
they were worth—100 livres were worth only
·36 of a livre. Exact facts about the advance
of the price level are not available, but it was
greatest in the rural districts, especially where
the revolutionary sentiments had made least
headway. In 1791 and 1792 inflation gave the
usual interim appearance of prosperity, but the
wild rise in prices made life very difficult for
those with fixed incomes, and for the working
classes. There were riots against the notes—the
salaries of officials were raised thirty times
without achieving the desired result. A judge
near Paris died of hunger. A pound of sugar was
sold for £450, and a pound of candles for £140. So
far as recent times are concerned, following the
Great War, we have history that is still fresh in
our minds. The figures are as follows :

1913	100
1918 December	352
1919 December	422
1920 April	587
1920 December	434
1921	325
1924	507
1925	632
1926 July	836
1927 October	587

You will see that by July 1926 France had reached a figure more than eight times the pre-war price level, and by a great effort this was reduced a year later to about six times, and then came the formal act of " Devaluation " at five times, when the franc formerly worth 10*d.* became worth 2*d.*, i.e. on a common gold-standard basis.

People who had borrowed what was worth one ounce of gold became entitled to repay with one-fifth of an ounce, and four-fifths of the national debt was virtually cancelled outright. Of course this was a formal recognition of what had already happened through the gradual rise in prices for anyone living in France. But to any lender from outside who had greater hopes of some day getting the equivalent of his loan, it was a real shock, and it will be fresh in your minds how representations were made by the British to the French Government concerning certain war loans to which the British had contributed, with a view of getting recognition of their original value, but without success—francs were francs, whatever change in their habits !

Why was it that there was such great inflation in France following upon the war ? First of all, there was a refusal to tax effectively in order to balance the budget. The French hate new taxation, and they were not fully alive to the dangers of inflation. For long enough they buoyed up their hopes of balancing their budget, with all its exceptional post-war expenditure, by expectation of large receipts from reparations. (The history of these reparations we will study later.) But as budget after budget was unbalanced, and as taxes fell more and more into arrear, so the causes of inflation became actively operative. The effect was increased by a flight from the franc, when large sums were invested in foreign centres. Moreover, the French actually incurred very large expenditure in rebuilding in the devastated areas in expectation of reparations, and so they not only failed to balance a normal budget, but they incurred expenditure on an exceptional budget quite unprovided with immediate receipts. " By shouting ' no ' to everything, Parliament had in effect whispered ' yes ' to the policy of inflation," says Professor Haig.

For it requires singularly little positive action to make inflation. And the average Frenchman repudiated the very thought of it. But failure to tax, and to balance budgets, in itself makes inflation inevitable, growing as it goes. When it got at last away from politics, into a committee of experts, they reported (July 1926) :

The fall of the franc has caused great ravages in our national economic life. It has continued the destruction of capital which the war had begun. The country believed that it was maintaining its spending capacity, whereas in reality it was consuming its own capital. No doubt trade and industry have experienced a period of apparent prosperity ; even as yet there is no unemployment, sales are easy, and exports active. Many Frenchmen live in a state of illusion ; in reality, in spite of nominally increased profits, there is in many cases an absence of real profit. The French are working and producing ; but most of them are becoming unconsciously poorer.

A few new fortunes have been created, but only too often they are the unhealthy and temporary fruit of currency depreciation. This depreciation gives debtors, by the automatic reduction of their debts, an easy way of becoming rich, but creditors grow weary, the spirit of saving disappears, credit becomes impossible and production is threatened.

In France, a country of the middle classes and of small-scale industrialisation, where prosperity is based on the capacity to save, the consequences of monetary instability are particularly serious. If thrift were to become the quality of fools, if the attractions of speculation and gambling were to take the place of productive labour, we should see before very long the disappearance of our national virtues. To safeguard the economic life of the country, the franc must be given the fundamental quality of a currency—stability.

So far it is clear how inflation comes about, what it is and what it does. Now what happens in the reverse direction ? That forms the subject of our third lecture.

III

A Cloak-room Analogy

We have seen that inflation takes place whenever
the means of purchasing, i.e. the tokens by
which purchasing takes place, are increased
more rapidly than production or the goods
capable of being purchased. True deflation is
really the exact opposite. The tickets that are
used, the tokens of purchase, become less and
less compared with production, and prices fall.
Shall we, by way of a crude illustration, consider
what may happen in the cloak-room of a picture
gallery, where there is a fairly regular attendance, which never gets beyond a certain point ?
The attendant has a number of little bone or
ivory tokens which he gives out to those people
who have handed in their umbrellas and various
other belongings before going into the gallery.
The number that he has is limited, but they have
always so far proved sufficient for the day's
work—he has never found himself without any
tokens at all, and he has no large surplus that
has never been used. Now let us suppose that
there is a vastly increased attendance. What will
happen ? Instead of five hundred visitors a day
there are now one thousand. Well, if they go in
and out very quickly, and only spend half the

time that the original five hundred spent, then very likely the attendant will handle the situation quite successfully with the existing supply of checks, for the "frequency" will have increased, and the number actually in the place at one time may be no greater than it was before. But this is rather an artificial assumption, and we have really to consider an actually increased *attendance*, by which we mean the presence of double the number of people in the place at any particular time. The first thing that the attendant would probably do is to put two articles upon one check, a trilby hat and a vanity bag belonging to a couple of friends or an umbrella and walking stick belonging to people who are obviously together. One check or one ticket would then represent two articles, which are handed in and taken out at the same time. Or, better still, if he has paper or cardboard checks, he might use another device—he might cut all his tickets in half, so that you might have the upper half of 518 and that would correspond with the upper half of 518 of the counterfoil, and some other visitor would have the lower half. He would double the effective use of his tickets by halving them all. As soon as he asks the authorities for a double allowance of checks his difficulties are over, and "one article one check" again becomes the rule. On the other hand, suppose that the authorities want to save expense. They might say to the cloak-room attendant, we must do with half the supply after this—you must put two or more articles on one check in future. Then they would be *deflating* in a definite sense. The case of double the visitors for the original number of checks is not usually called deflation, although the effect is the same.

Deflation either by less Money or more Goods

These various devices are just a kind of parable of what happens when deflation takes place, and when a single note, we will say for a £ or a dollar. does double duty, i.e. buys twice as much, or prices are half what they were. So our store-keeper for the national heap has many vouchers going backwards and forwards, and if they have been in the past just enough to keep the heap moving out in consumption equally with pro-duction, then we have to suppose that, if he has no means of increasing them, but the goods on the heap or the size of the heap were to double, he would be in the same kind of difficulty as the attendant in the cloak-room. Now, everyone is bringing *more* goods per person to the production heap, or there are *more* people bringing the same each, and yet the storekeeper has to do his work with the same number of vouchers ; he now finds that his tickets are not so plentiful as the goods, and so they have to do greater service. When they are given to the producer or the person who has a right to something upon the heap—when they are giving him his right to take something off—they have to do duty for a larger quantity of goods.

But there is another way in which deflation takes place. You will remember that in our original conception of the heap, we imagined the Government or the collective State to be taking a number of the tickets (that belonged to individuals and that gave individuals a title to the heap) and using them themselves, as a State, or as we might put it, "absorbing purchasing power" by taxation, and having the right as a government to buy that part of the national heap which the taxed individuals no longer can take. In considering inflation, we imagined the Government not getting hold of enough of the heap for its purpose by the tickets that it absorbs by taxation, and having to print more. Now we have the reverse operation. The Government may absorb by taxation a number of the tickets *and never use them.* That is to say, the tickets are never presented to the storekeeper, but are torn up. If the central bank had previously created money for the Government, and the loan is now repaid and the " creation " reversed, this is what we call " paying off debt," when that is done out of taxation and not new borrowing. The quantity of goods remains what it was before, but the number of vouchers has been reduced, and so there are not enough presented to clear off the whole heap. More goods on the heap, therefore, go out ultimately for every voucher that is presented, i.e. prices fall, for you can get twice as many goods away from the heap for one voucher as you could before, and the price of one unit is only half a voucher, instead of a whole voucher.

Now, when people pay off loans to the bank and the bank does not lend the proceeds to others, it may alter the total quantity of " purchasing power " as we call it, and the ratio between the total vouchers in the hands of the public and the bank's resources, and there are various other devices by which deflation may take place, not through the Government and taxation, but through the quantity of purchasing power which the central bank allows to be out in the country.

The Record of Deflation

That is enough for the theory of deflation for the moment. Now, does deflation happen ? Did it happen, after the war ? Look at our own British price level first of all. I have shown you that we reached our high point in April 1920. Now look at the course of index numbers on prices after that :—

Price level

1913	. . .	100		
1920 April	. .	325	⎫	
1920 December	.	263	⎬ Fall of almost 50 per cent.	
1921 July	. .	194	⎭	
1921 December	.	167·9	⎫	
1922 ,,	.	155·8	⎬ Relative stability.	
1923 ,,	.	163·4	⎭	
1924 ,,	.	166·2	⎫	
			Going on the gold standard.	
1925	. . .	159		
1926	. . .	148	⎬ 35 points since December 1924	
1927	. . .	141	= 20 per cent. " gold defla-	
1928	. . .	140	tion."	
1929	. . .	136·5		
1930	. . .	119·5	The great slump.	
1931 September	.	99·2	⎫ " Off the gold standard."	
1931 December	.	105·8	⎭	

You will see that from the high point in April 1920 to December 1921 the price level practically halved. Then it remained remarkably stable for the next three years to September 1924. Although it was not a gold standard price level, it was actually more stable on the whole for a time than the dollar in America. Shortly after that, in 1925, we went back to the gold standard, and from that time there has been a deflation of gold prices, and by January 1930 it had reached 131, a decline of 34 points since December 1924, or a deflation, i.e. a fall of over 20 per cent. After that date, by September 1931, when we went off the gold standard, it fell a further 24 per cent.

Deflation and Gold

I can hear you exclaim at once, " But you have been talking about paper money, printed notes and all that kind of thing—tickets that can be produced and destroyed at will. How can deflation possibly happen when there is a fixed currency related to gold ? " If gold were the only currency, and there were no notes, so that nothing was ever bought and sold unless gold passed with it, then we should have the most exact relationship, and the only way in which deflation of prices could happen would be when there was a vast decrease in the quantity of gold mined and used as currency compared with the quantity of goods produced. If these quantities varied very much either more or less, you would get inflation and deflation respectively, in a most

direct way. But it is not usual to apply the
terms deflation and inflation to a variation in
the quantity of gold used as direct purchasing
power, and the *only form* of purchasing power.
For in practice currency and purchasing power
are made up, not only of gold, but also paper
based on a certain reserve of gold, and, as a
matter of fact, the quantity of money that is
being used as purchasing power is not the same
as the quantity of gold, which varies in different
countries.

When we say that a country has a "ratio
of 40 per cent." we mean broadly that for
every 40 units of gold it possesses it is entitled
to issue 100 units of purchasing power. Let
us suppose that it runs short of purchasing
power—short of tickets or checks—compared
with the production of goods. As one way out of
its difficulty, it might very easily alter the ratio,
and declare that instead of a ratio of 40 it shall
be 20 per cent. Immediately it is entitled to
have for its 40 units of gold not 100, but 200
units of purchasing power. This would, obviously, be inflation if there were no change in
the quantity of goods, but if the quantity of
goods had doubled the result would be to keep
prices the same. Supposing that the actual
quantity of goods to be purchased were doubled,
but the ratio is not altered and the quantity of
gold is not altered, then we should have deflation, because prices would be compelled to drop.
Now, let us suppose that our original quantity

6

of 40 units of gold is doubled, because gold comes into the country for one reason or another, and we still retain our ratio of 40 per cent., and thus increase our total purchasing power from 100 to 200. Then if we get an increase of goods not merely double but four times as much, we should still have the *effect* of deflation. Prices would fall, and this ratio between purchasing power and production might be in itself connected with the quantity of gold. Therefore, it is quite possible to have " gold deflation," and this is what has been happening throughout the world on a very extensive scale. The quantity of gold that is available for use as the basis of purchasing power depends on the quantity mined, and it depends also on the quantity that is put away, and by " put away " I mean absorbed in jewellery or in the arts or put in a stocking, but not used at all as the basis of purchasing power. But there are more ways of " putting money away," or hoarding, than putting it in teapots and chimneys, or even putting it in gold rings round the ankles of Indian women ! If the banks have very large reserves compared with what they have normally, or if they let their " ratio " become much higher than usual and only issue notes fully backed by gold in their vaults, then they are hoarding too, so that there are various kinds of hoarding—the hoarding of a French peasant, the hoarding of an Indian peasant, the hoarding of a bank with modern and advanced ideas.

The Varying Proportion of Credit

There is an even more striking method of securing inflation and deflation, and that is when the quantity of individual *credit*, as distinct from public notes, that is allowed to be based upon a given quantity of gold varies greatly. This amount is not fixed—sometimes and in some countries the amount issued is very much greater than at other times and in other places. Imagine credit as a kind of picture that is made by a pantagraph. You have seen that interesting little toy, where you pass a pointer over all the lines of a picture and the pencil at the end of a long arm rigidly connected with your pointer makes an exactly similar picture two or three or four times as large, according to the size of the pantagraph and the length of the arm upon which you have put the pencil. But whatever the size it is always in strict proportion, and the picture will be reproduced on that scale so long as you keep the fixed arm length. But the pantagraph of credit is not a fixed arm—it is, so to speak, an elastic one, sometimes longer and sometimes shorter. You will see now something of what is meant by deflation, and why, when there has been inflation such as we had in Russia and in Germany in recent years, it is almost impossible to deflate after such astronomical figures of inflation—one can only wipe out the currency altogether and start afresh.

When Deflation is Impossible

The assignats of the French Revolution were of course not " deflated "—they just passed out as annihilated. They were succeeded by a new currency of much smaller dimensions, and the redemption of assignats was prescribed at the rate of thirty to one of the new notes. But these fell to 2·5 per cent. of their face value. In 1797 gold was introduced at 1 franc for 100 of the notes and 3,000 of the assignats. The various debts of the inflation period were valued on the basis of local tables according to local prices which had varied greatly. But " enormous suffering was inflicted on large numbers of people at various stages of this disastrous experiment ; and the Government itself incurred colossal losses by the discharge in depreciated paper of obligations contracted towards it in coin." [1] During the process of replacing assignats by specie, unemployment became a real ground of discontent, and it had never been a complaint while the assignats were mounting up. Wage contracts were not easily adapted to a monetary unit which depreciated by half every two or three months,[2] so that commercial contracts fell into even greater chaos.

It might be thought that if tremendous harm is done whenever there is inflation, then doing the reverse, that is deflating, must do tremendous good. But the evils of deflation, particularly

---

[1] *Cambridge Modern History*, vol. viii.
[2] Hawtrey, *Econ. Journ.*, 1918, p. 311.

rapid deflation, are very nearly as great as those of inflation. The truth is that only stable values really do justice in a complicated society.

Did Germany Deflate ?

Germany did not really deflate in the ordinary sense of the word—she annihilated the old currency and started afresh, and since she started afresh there has been no conspicuous change in the price level, except so far as it has come down with the general world price level on the *basis of gold deflation*. The level went from 156 to 134, and back to 144 in 1929—not in itself enough to do any serious social damage.

You have seen, in the last lecture, how, under the regime of inflation, all the old fixed debts were practically wiped out for nothing. Those which had not actually been repaid would under the returning process of deflation gradually have become greater and greater in their purchasing power, though never of course getting back to their original value, and the greatest inequality would have existed between those who had borrowed money at late periods of inflation with a high price level and those who had either borrowed money earlier or repaid their borrowing. But they were wiped out altogether, and when the new currency was started something had to be done about them. There was a great agitation for the " valorisation " of old debts. So there were elaborate provisions made for giving them a certain definite value, though nothing

like their original value—something about 15
per cent. in the new currency compared with
the old. The old war debts were allowed to rank
for something like a sixth or seventh of their
original equivalent in goods.

Deflation in France

In France the story of deflation is much more
clearly seen. The price level reached the high
point of 836 in July 1929 at a time when there
was practically a panic about the rate of foreign
exchange. But by regaining confidence and by
tackling the budget systematically and firmly
they got it back to 587 by October 1927. The
fall of the franc caused great ravages in their
national economic life. It continued the destruction of capital which the war had begun.

What they wanted to stay the tide of inflation and to turn
the tide was a strong government which would not be afraid
of the measures of taxation that were necessary. Herriot
fell, and when Poincaré succeeded him there was confidence
that the tide would turn. He was able to persuade the
French people that four-fifths of the franc *could not be saved*,
and in so doing he saved the other fifth. Unfortunately, as
you know, while the consequences were not felt severely in
France, there was a great grievance amongst foreigners
who had debts due to them in French currency.

" As to the rate of stabilisation, the experts
rejected the idea of complete revalorisation.
Such a procedure would involve continuous and
systematic deflation which would be ruinous to
the taxpayer, as well as to industry, trade and

agriculture, on account of the necessity of lowering prices indefinitely, and of keeping to contracts made in times of monetary depreciation."[1]

The Cause of Deflation

Deflation is only necessary because of prior inflation, which cannot be held at a fixed point but must go ever upwards. It arises either because there is a definite desire to link the currency to the gold or silver currencies of the world at a general level, or because the economic consequences of inflation can be offset and corrected before they become too set. If injustice to wage earners and interest receivers is proceeding with great rapidity by rising prices, there is a strong impetus to bring back the situation to one which is reasonable before it is too late.

Over the centuries there is a kind of secular and imperceptible inflation which is not usually called by that name. The succeeding generations of active and business men continually reduce a little the advantages of the savings of the dead, and reduce the inheritors' portions. So purchasing power, by modern credit devices, has outrun even increased producing power in the long view.

But in the shorter view, wars and revolutions have been the prime cause of rapid inflation, and have necessitated either a completely new beginning or else a prolonged period of deflation

[1] Haig, *Public Finance of Post-war France.*

in each case. A recent American writer says :
" The destruction wrought by great wars is not
confined to the fields of battle. A more lasting
imprint is left on the economic life of later
generations, and in no respect is this aftermath
of war more certain or more uniform than in
the course of prices."

Deflation in the United States

The experience of the United States when
expressed in graphic form shows a singular
uniformity of pattern for the Napoleonic, the
Civil and the World Wars. At the first the
index rose from round about 80 to 125 in two or
three years, and then declined 58 per cent. in the
twenty-nine years between 1814 and 1843 to
below 60. In the Civil War it rose instantly
from about 60 to 130, and from 1864 for
thirty-two years declined (by 65 per cent.)
to a point well below the 60 mark. During
the World War it jumped from about 65 to about
155, and fell in the following ten years to about
80, and a continuation of the " pattern " of the
previous curves would bring it slowly down to
60 in the next twenty years. The greater part of
the price deflation in each case occurs in the first
few years. Thus in *half* the decline period, after
1814, seven-eighths of the amount of decline
took effect ; after 1864 in fifteen years, 82½
per cent. of the extra range from high and low
was registered. The lesson drawn by the American writer is that the greater part of the " 1920

and onwards " decline has now been experienced, but he is unduly optimistic as to the progress of business during the remaining period of slowly falling prices that he postulates.

Advantages and Disadvantages

Deflation has the initial advantage that it obviates the realisation of impending grievances due to that part of the preceding inflation which has not been " absorbed " in a new and adjusted range of money wages and debts. But as soon as deflation touches a point at which the various factors of production are receiving real rewards which are reasonably just to them all, and enable them all to function at their highest efficiency, its good work is done. If it proceeds below this point it has the following grave disadvantages :

(*a*) It gives interest receivers and loanholders an increasing and unnecessary proportion of the natural production at the expense of enterprise and risk-taking businesses.

(*b*) It gives the wage earners a greater real reward than they are producing, and leads to efforts to reduce money wages and prevent real wages from rising. This provokes industrial unrest and interruption of production.

(*c*) It produces unemployment and a heavy budget contribution to relieve it, with a consequential increase in taxation on a falling body of profits.

(*d*) By the operation of the foregoing it seriously depresses business enterprise. If a business produces 100 units for £100 and pays out £80 for interest on debentures and wages, and then has £20 as the reward for risk upon the ordinary capital, it may be just worth while to carry on or even extend the business. But when prices fall 25 per cent. it receives £75 instead of £100, and having still to pay away £80 it loses £5, and has no incentive to expand, and no credit to enable it to borrow. In due course it loses its existing funds and becomes bankrupt.

(*e*) It makes the burden of the national debt unduly heavy and even impossible to bear, and redistributes the national income so that the stresses on different parts are uneconomic.

(*f*) It wastes savings, because these are not properly employed in new investments.

Deflation is the result of prior inflation, but its evils are the consequence of the fact that the money payments made within economic society are not equally fluid and changeable, and because the mainspring of that society is the profitability of business.

IV

" Reparation " and " War Indemnity " are often regarded as equivalent terms, but strictly they may mean quite distinct things. Reparation really means what is wanted to repair damage, or to make good, while indemnity may mean a fine which is a compensation for war and a " profit " to the victor. But in the case of the last war, inasmuch as any estimate of the total of the actual damage was always far in excess of what Germany could pay, the question of any surplus above such a figure as a net " profit " to the victors never arose, and the term indemnity has fallen into disuse. The conquerors in history have usually taken away their booty in produce, and kind, and slaves, and that booty was in itself the cause of many early wars. They " lived on the land," and often the reward of success was the retention of territory.

The French Indemnity 1871

The most famous example of an " indemnity " —for the word " reparation " (now often rather clumsily called " reparations ") acquired a special meaning after the last war—is that of France in 1871. An indemnity of 200 million sterling was imposed and liquidated in less than two years and four months. It is not correct to suppose that the French really, by their own economy, achieved this. Various means were adopted. First, they gave up a railway in Alsace-Lorraine which had been started, and the French Government had to settle with its owners in their own bonds. Then they collected a good sum of German money left in France by the German army and transferred over 20 million £ in gold and silver. The rest was transferred in foreign bills of exchange, and to get these the French Government borrowed the bills and investments from its citizens, and gave them its own in exchange. The French Government really borrowed practically all the funds required for the indemnity by floating two large bond issues equal to 230 million £. It is not possible to say how much the French really tightened their belts to buy bonds and how far they used up past savings. It has been estimated that the public bought 60 million £ out of current savings or hoards. But taxes were not increased sufficiently to cover even the increased interest charges for these bonds, so the increase in the public debt was permanent. No special difficulties arose in international trade, and France had a favourable balance during the period.

Indemnities in the Great War

The difference between Germany and ourselves on this subject during the war was remarkable, for they definitely held off imposing heavy taxa-

tion in expectation of an indemnity, and relied
upon it, whereas we were careful not to anticipate such a source of strength. In the same
way, since the war we have not taken such
payments seriously into account for our budgets,
but France has relied upon them to balance her
budgets.

In the fever that followed the Armistice there
were two main cries : " Hang the Kaiser " and
" Make Germany pay." Anyone who ventured to
express any moderation or doubt was quickly
put down as pro-German or lacking in patriotism. The road to popularity on the platform was
vehemence on this subject. Indeed, it had no
little political significance, and the Government
were criticised for not making it sufficiently clear
that they were not going to " let the Hun off."
As Mr. Keynes said, " Mr. Hughes was evoking a
good deal of attention by his demands for a very
large indemnity, and Lord Northcliffe was lending his powerful aid." This enabled Mr. Lloyd
George to kill two birds with one stone and drown
both critics. Mr. Barnes, a member of the War
Cabinet, and representing labour, said, " I am
for hanging the Kaiser." At the election a
Times correspondent reported, " It is the candi-
date who deals with the issue of debt, who adopts
Mr. Barnes's phrase about hanging the Kaiser,
and plumps for the payment of the cost of the
war by Germany, who rouses his audience and
strikes the notes to which they are most respon-
sive." The high-water mark was reached by Sir

Eric Geddes in a reaction against a suspicion that he was not thoroughgoing on the subject : " We will get out of her all you can squeeze out of a lemon, and a bit more—squeeze her until you can hear the pips squeak." The real demand settled down shortly to the " whole cost of the war." The higher this cost was put the more popular the speaker.

Officials and economists were modest, and their figures ranged from 2,000 million £ upwards, but politicians, bankers and lawyers gave 20,000 million £, as well as property and colonies. A very long wrangle took place in the Conference, and a large slice of the time taken on the Treaty was given to this subject. Germany was made liable for all damage done to the civilian population of the Allied and associated powers and to their property during the period of the belligerency of each by aggression by land, by sea and from the air. It was soon agreed that this covered injury to persons and dependents, acts of cruelty and violence to the civilians, and damage to property. But the chief discussion came over pensions and separation allowances. The Treaty never really faced the problem of Germany's capacity to pay, but laid down the subjects of her liability, and left it to an impartial tribunal to determine what the amount of this bill was. No one really answered the question, " What can Germany pay ? " for the Treaty said, in effect, Germany ought to meet this kind of bill, which it is not our business to compute in money ; and the Reparation Commission said, " We are not responsible for the items, we have only to do the sum and this is the answer." When the result was published at 6,600 million £ it did not shock people, for they had become used to hearing about such large figures. Mr. Klotz, in September 1919, estimated the total claims against Germany as 15,000 million £, and figures as high as 24,000 million £ had been mentioned by responsible people.

Much more important than these astronomical figures was the programme laid down by the Treaty for the actual annual payments towards the final liability : 1,000 million £ before May 1921, and bonds for 2,000 million £ by the same date, bearing interest, with very heavy annual payments in lieu, say 75 million £ from 1921 to 1925 and 180 million £ annually after. Then came further bonds, until the whole of the bill as fixed by the Commission should be paid.

I am reminded of the story of the lecturer on astronomy in a village hall, who said that the sun would be extinct in a hundred million years and our own world a frozen globe. At the end he invited questions and observations, and a yokel at the back got up and asked anxiously : " Do you mind repeating what you said about the sun drying up ? " The lecturer did so. " Oh," exclaimed the yokel, obviously much relieved, " a hundred million years ! I thought you said a

million." I think people were in much the same
state of mind as regards these tables, and, at any
rate, they showed no signs of fearing what might
happen if the figures were wrong—just a little
extra inconvenience for Germany perhaps ; but
if you had tried to promulgate the idea then that
any material mistake in the figures would be
disastrous also for the creditors and involve
them in financial collapse, you would have been
laughed to scorn as a theorist.

The economists and officials said from the
beginning that these sums were impossible, and
Mr. Keynes's book, *The Economic Consequences
of the Peace*, is well worth reading to-day on this
point. But lawyers and bankers were more in
favour than economists, because they promised
more and did not make absurd difficulties.
They were not guided by the French indemnity
of 1871, for on a like parallel the burden would
have been between 500 and 600 million £, and
France was not exhausted in 1871 to the same
extent as Germany in 1919.

The Elementary Principles

When a country has paid all that it can pay
by direct means, such as a transfer of gold and
securities, ships, and property in ceded territory,
it can only pay in its production of goods and
services duly transferred as exports. It cannot
pay any more gold unless it has gold mines,
though, of course, it can get gold from other
countries first, and then pass it to the creditor,

but that means exports too. If the countries of
the world do not want extra imports and put up
their tariffs, then they make it very difficult for
the debtor to pay at all. We have spent twelve
weary years trying to dodge this uncomfortable
dilemma, and we are still face to face with the
same impossibilities—twelve weary years in an
infinite struggle in endless series of conferences,
gradually cutting down, bit by bit, these fantastic totals. Germany was absolutely denuded
of working capital and exhausted by war, and
she had not the ghost of a chance upon this
programme from the very outset. The immediate
demands were too extreme.

Germany's Annual Task

It was one thing to settle the total amount of
Germany's liability, and however wrong the *total*
might be it could not lead to immediate disaster ;
but it was quite another to say how much
Germany was to pay *every year*. For obviously,
when the question of interest enters in, the burden may be, according to the length of time
taken, very much heavier than the face value of
the debt. After numerous conferences at all
kinds of places, the figures finally settled down
into something like an actual programme, in
what was known as the London Settlement in
May 1921. Here there was a scheme for deliver-
ing bonds or definite promises for future payment (with which I will not bother you), and also
a scheme of payment year by year. Germany had

7

to pay, until her total liability was discharged, a hundred million sterling a year, and also a sum equivalent to 26 per cent. of the value of her exports. This was a kind of elastic figure which would measure her prosperity, and, on any reasonable measure of exports that were likely, it represented a less total burden than the original demands of the Treaty, amounting to 138 milliard gold marks. These sums had to be paid in quarterly instalments. The long and painful process of reducing Germany's liability gradually had begun.

When Lord Cunliffe had been making his estimates and the figures had been given out in the British general election just immediately after the war, the figure expressed in terms of an annuity represented 1,440 million £ a year, well over half the national income of Britain before the war. The forecast in the French Chamber nearly a year later brought it down to 900 millions ; the assessment by the Reparation Commission in April 1921 brought it down to about 414 millions a year, and this London Settlement on any reasonable aspect, such as was given by Mr. Keynes at the time, was 230 million £ per annum. Mr. Keynes had estimated in 1919 the figure at 100 million £, at the same time as the French Chamber were considering 900 million £. At the time of the conference the British and French Prime Ministers would not accept a lower figure in meeting the pressure put upon them by the Americans than 500 million £, say, two and a half times the amount which they had to accept a little less than two years later under the pressure of emerging hard facts.

The position created by the 26 per cent. upon exports being payable as reparations was absurd from the beginning. The moment Germany was successful in paying, by an export surplus, the amount required of her, she had an additional burden through this 26 per cent., and then when she was successful in making that new amount up, she had a 26 per cent. upon that, and so on. Germany started off all right with the instalment for August 1921, paid out of foreign balances which she had already accumulated for the purpose. Her November instalment was covered by deliveries of coal and other materials. Mr. Keynes estimated that the instalments of January and February 1922 would be covered out of further deliveries and advances and the foreign assets of Germany, if the German Government could get hold of them from her subjects. But he anticipated great difficulty in April 1922, while the further instalments were clearly likely to put Germany absolutely " in the soup." Mr. Keynes said, " Some time between February and August 1922 Germany will succumb to an inevitable default. This is the maximum extent of our breathing space." He first published this forecast in August 1921 ; it was extraordinarily close to the truth—by the end of 1922 Germany was falling into arrear and the French were making preparations to occupy the Ruhr. As Germany got into difficulties people were more and more suspicious that she was following a policy of " ca'canny," to use a term from the labour world.

Looking back upon the circumstances, the utmost we can say is that having been given an impossible task to perform, she saw ahead of her the kind of disaster that was inevitable, and did nothing towards the end to resist that inevitability or to delay it. The occupation of the Ruhr by the French, and the removal of it completely from German economic life, was like cutting the heart and the nerve centre out of a great organism. It completely undermined her taxpaying capacity and her administrative machinery, and made some kind of inflation almost inevitable. Once having embarked on the inflation ramp, as we have seen, she could not stop herself. Most people were then genuinely convinced that there was bad faith on Germany's part. There were all kinds of small items of evidence to give support to this idea, but, taking any large view, it is quite obvious that what happened was only a question of time. When all the foreign investments that are available have been given up—and remember it is one thing for an individual in a country to own foreign investments, and quite another thing for a government to discover them and obtain them in order to hand them over—when all the gold that has been accumulated has gone, we have only two methods left. The first is a definite export of goods, either direct—what we call, deliveries in kind—actually arranged to be accepted by the creditor government and used either by the Government itself or sold by it to its subjects, or secondly, an export surplus in the ordinary course of trade—a "favourable trade balance" —an excess of goods and services sent out over those brought in. Beyond that the only possible method is that of loans. The history of reparations has been very largely a question of lending back to Germany, not directly, but through the ordinary courses of investment from abroad, very much the sums that she has owed, and this was absolutely essential in Germany's case for some time, because she was so completely denuded of circulating capital. Germany was required to produce a big national heap somehow or other, and to take from it this large sum of over 200 million £ worth a year and to get foreign countries, not necessarily the actual creditors, to accept it.

Now, it is one thing for a foreign government to accept the proceeds of such sales when they have been made, but it is quite another thing to sell the goods to individuals, for the moment the individuals feel the competition of German goods in their own industries, then of course they want tariffs raised. The whole history of reparations has been a fight by the politicians to get paid, and a fight by the industrialists to prevent themselves being paid. If all the countries had been willing to accept German goods without tariffs, the task would have been difficult enough ; it meant definitely that the German workpeople must have a lower standard of life, because they were only entitled to what was left on the heap after paying reparations, or they must have longer hours of work in order to have the same sized heap as other people and something more to spare for this purpose. But as fast as there was any attempt to do this we had international movements, such as the Washington Conference, to equate all the hours of labour in the different countries, Germany not excluded. So that in effect we told Germany she was to produce all this extra amount, but that we would not take it except through tariffs barriers, and she wasn't to produce it by longer hours ; also, if she paid lower wages, i.e. if she took the amount of goods required out of her people's consumption, then the tariffs were put up, particularly on the American principle, which seeks to " equalise the cost of production " and to make good the difference between a foreign standard of wage and the home standard. So in every possible way a check was put, unconsciously no doubt, upon Germany's ability to discharge her debt.

As I say, the task was a difficult one in any event, because Germany has highly specialised manufactures, many of which people do not want in unlimited quantities. There is a principle in economics called " elasticity of demand," which shows that when we have had as much as we want of a thing for ordinary purposes, we will only take more in preference to something else if we can get it at a very much lower price, and there will come a point at which we shall not take more at any price. You can well do with one piano in a house—conceivably if they are very cheap, you might have a second, but more than that would be a perfect nuisance. Even with toys—every family can have enough and be satiated with them, and so you can only market an additional or extra large quantity to a particular market at very low prices. Now, it is the total price that tells in reparations, not the total goods, and it might well be that, in order to double the amount of money exports, you would have to treble or quadruple the amount of the actual goods exported, because of this " elasticity of demand."

I will not describe further the terrible mess into which the whole German economic organisation was brought by depreciation of her currency, through the forced purchases of foreign currencies and their effect upon the exchanges, and through the occupation of the Ruhr.

The Idea of Capacity to Pay

In these earlier days, when people were talking about what Germany could pay, they nearly always thought of it in terms of the burden of taxation that she could bear, or a comparison of her total wealth with that of other people. It was only the professional economists who really recognised that if Germany could not produce a trade balance, i.e. a surplus of exports over imports, her foreign exchanges were bound to go wrong and react upon her currency. When the excessive pressure upon Germany and her exchanges had thoroughly disintegrated all her financial systems and led to the Ruhr occupation, you will remember that at the end of 1923 the Dawes Committee was set up. This Committee was primarily intended to make recommendations to balance the German budget. It was not allowed in set terms to have anything to do with reparations ; that was altogether too tender a spot for our French friends at the time, for it was supposed to be an interference with the Treaty. Anything which even remotely questioned the total of the reparations to be paid would have, at that time, been quite impossible diplomatically. Now, a budget cannot be kept balanced unless currency is assured of reasonable stability, and unless the exchanges are functioning properly. A budget cannot, then, be balanced, or arrangements made for it to be balanced, unless the liability for reparations annually to be met out of it is a known figure. It was therefore quickly found that the terms of reference of the Committee could not possibly be dealt with satisfactorily unless the reparations question *as an annual burden* was faithfully treated, although the total burden, that is, the number of years for which it would be paid, was not so important.

The first thing that the Committee did was quite new in the popular treatment of the subject. It was to distinguish between the tax burden that the German people could bear as such and the amount of money or export surplus that could be got out of the country without deranging the exchanges—two connected questions, but not two identical amounts. The principles governing the determination of the maximum in each case are quite different. If any attempt is made to export as reparations more goods than have been extracted from the producers by taxation, then trouble is bound to ensue. But it was an open question to many people whether once having got possession of the goods by taxation, the Government could persuade the consumers and producers of other countries to take them. The Dawes Committee said: "Let the Government raise the requisite taxes to a specified amount, such as is capable of being borne in a balanced budget. Let Germany discharge her obligation in her own currency in marks, and leave it to the creditors to arrange to get those marks out of Germany and turned into the currency of the other countries without damaging German credit." Accordingly they were not dogmatic as to the amount of export surplus, or whatever other method might be effective for getting the marks expressed in the wealth of other countries. But they set up a special committee to supervise the transfer of marks into dollars, francs and sterling, and to stop transferring at any moment when it was likely to endanger the stability of the German currency. What was likely to endanger it ? Only unwillingness of foreign consumers to buy German goods to the requisite extent at the prices profitable to German producers. Then there were not enough pounds, francs, etc., for Germany to hand over to the British, French and other Governments, at the same time as they handed the marks got by taxation in Germany to the German producers for their goods.

Some of the Powers were very keen on deliveries in kind, i.e. actual arrangements for transporting over the border physical objects, coal and the like, and they were so dependent upon this at the time that, however necessary it was to give a breathing space to Germany during her crisis, these sums or deliveries had to be maintained. The Committee made it quite clear that essentially the deliveries did not differ from money obligations in their effect upon the exchanges. It was considered that it would take practically five years for Germany to reach anything like a normal condition again, and therefore her obligations were " stepped up," as it were, quite gradually, till the normal year, the fifth year, was reached, when the burden was to be 125 million sterling per annum. Now you will see that this is the annual interest on about 2,500 millions of capital, whereas the actual debt under the Treaty was in the neighbourhood of 6,600 million £. Therefore, with a payment each

year of 125 millions, Germany was really not
actually paying anything *off* the capital at all,
and the debt would therefore go on accumulating
and getting bigger in perpetuity ! This was impossible as a permanent solution.

But the Dawes Committee were not empowered
to touch reparations at all. Therefore they had
to leave the question of the total debt in the air,
and the annuity that they settled upon did not
really touch the capital of the debt itself, except
for one possibility. There was a provision that
the 125 million £ a year should be increased pro-
gressively as Germany's power to pay increased,
and that increased power to pay was to be settled
by reference to an " index of production " made
up of various factors, showing how German
wealth and annual income and population were
increasing. Obviously, if this index mounted at
a rapid rate, then some day the annuity might
be sufficient to pay off more than the interest
and touch the capital, but this was a rather
remote possibility.

The Dawes Committee said they were paying proper attention to the principle that
Germany should be called upon to bear a
tax burden at least as heavy as that of her
creditors. As a matter of fact, merely as a tax
burden, to a country with the population and
wealth of Germany, the reparation schedule
laid down in the Dawes Plan was not at all
excessive. It had a definite meaning then as a
proportion of her total production or national

heap, which all could understand and which was quite compassable. But, after all, it was not expressed as such a proportion—for example, as 5 per cent. of the goods she produced; it was expressed as a *money* burden, and if the prices of goods were to fall then the amount of goods covered by any given sum of money was correspondingly greater. So we might have found that with a very heavy fall in prices the total quantity of goods to be absorbed by Germany's creditors as their imports would go up very greatly, and it would be a very much heavier burden upon Germany's total production. If prices fell to one half, the burden would become 10 per cent., instead of 5. Provision was made against this possible contingency by a " gold clause," which provided that when the normal year came, in five years' time, if prices should be altered by 10 per cent., and if Germany's burden by a measure of price should be thus heavier than was intended, then the money amount should be adjusted downwards to produce the same result in total goods. Under this provision in the last two or three years the amount of the German money annuity would have been very heavily reduced.

The Sequel to the Dawes Plan

The contribution of the Dawes Plan was to re-establish German currency, and to make it clear to the world that there was a difference between taxable capacity and exporting capacity. It was

recognised that in the long run, as Germany
had no gold mines or foreign investments left,
reparations must be paid in goods and services,
additional to what would ordinarily have been
sent in exchange for her imports. But Germany's
export trade balance had never been great, and
it was a matter of great dispute amongst the
business experts how far the trade balance could
be increased. Some said that whatever was taken
away from the people by the Government by
taxation could come across the exchanges by
the ordinary processes of economic forces into
other countries without exceptional difficulty,
and no exchange difficulties need arise. Others
said that there were definite economic limits,
owing to the similarity of the chief creditors in
their manufactures, and owing to their tariffs,
and to Germany's capacity to export, and that
some day or other, especially when loans to
Germany ceased to be made freely, the Transfer
Committee would have to stop exchanging marks
into other currencies. It was thought that that
would be a terrible thing for Germany, because
it would interfere with her normal credit, and
her ordinary lenders for commercial purposes
would take fright, while perhaps even those who
had made loans in the past would find those
loans standing at a discount. In general, it was
thought possible that the very sign of action
by the Transfer Committee to prevent trouble
might precipitate a psychological and financial
crisis.

During these three or four years after the
Dawes Plan the world was full of speculation as
to what Germany's ultimate producing power
and exporting power might be. Few faced up to
the fact that the real problem was the ultimate
absorbing and importing power of her creditors.
Many thought that by the process of triangular
trade in undeveloped countries the matter could
be satisfactorily disposed of. I made a long
report to the International Chamber of Commerce in 1925, in which I showed the difficulties
of such a large trade balance being achieved by
Germany, without special assistance and co-
operation by her creditors, and sketched out a
theory of " assisted schemes " whereby large
sums of German wealth could be successfully
exported without raising difficulties unduly
amongst domestic manufacturers in their respective countries. During this period a great
deal of surplus wealth was being made in
America and elsewhere, and surplus savings were
seeking an outlet in the borrowing markets of
Europe. Germany found little difficulty, therefore, in securing loans from New York and from
London ; in fact, she had the money pressed upon
her. It may be said that during this reconstruction period the reparation payments were really
lent back to Germany, though not necessarily
by the countries who were accepting the reparations payments. The Agent-General in Berlin
continually warned the world that Germany was
borrowing too freely and was not investing the

money in reproductive assets. He felt, and the Germans felt, that all this alien political machinery within Germany to look after the matter and take the responsibility was unsatisfactory and provisional.

Before the normal or fifth year of the Dawes Plan had arrived, he had already proclaimed that it was high time that Germany should be given a definite task to discharge on her own responsibility, although many people thought that the time was not yet ripe for taking another step, and that Germany's capacity should be fully tested in a normal year and the machinery of the Dawes Plan put into action. But others considered that it was indeed time for the political machine to be removed from Germany, and that another attempt should be made to put the whole problem more into the commercial and less into the political field. Moreover, Germany's credit could never really be satisfactory until the total burden of reparations, and not merely the annual burden, was known. In 1929 the Young Plan came into being. It abolished the Transfer Committee, the Agent-General in Berlin, and all the political machinery, and laid down a schedule of payments to discharge the whole of a reduced total debt extending for a period of fifty-eight years.

Reparations and Debts

All this time it became a cardinal principle with the European creditors that the reparations due from Germany should be as nearly as possible " matched up " to the debts due to the United States. It was thought that in this way American attention might be drawn to the fact that the major part of what Germany was paying ultimately found its way into America. In the American Debt Settlement there is no provision for the changing value of gold and the tremendous increase of burdens that might come about with a world-wide fall in prices. Therefore this provision in the Dawes Plan was dropped completely, and in the Young Plan " matched up with the debts " meant that the whole scheme was fully at the mercy of the changing value of gold.

The Young Plan divided the German annuity into two parts—the first part being something that was payable unconditionally whatever the state of German finance, and that could be issued as a public loan to the public in the respective countries to which it was due. Public opinion has always sharply distinguished between a debt between two governments and one between a government and foreign individual lenders, for the last has been thought to be much less subject to politics. It is thought that the German Government would not dare to default in interest to a French or English citizen, because it would spoil her commercial credit too. So if the French Government are entitled to receive, say, 50 million francs annually as an unconditional annuity, they can " mobilise " it or float a loan to their citizens for, say, 1,000 million francs, on which the 50 million is the interest. They can then use the proceeds to pay off other national debt. The effect is to transfer the interest burden from their own taxpayers to the German taxpayers.

The second part of the German payment was the "conditional annuity" which might be suspended for a period of years after certain preliminaries had been observed, and this was intended to tide Germany over any period of great depression of trade. There was a special Advisory Committee attached to the Bank for International Settlements, which was to say what should be done in such circumstances. The Reparation Commission and all the other political machinery of the old reparations schemes were scrapped, but this new institution, called the Bank for International Settlements, was created.

This bank had as one of its primary responsibilities the receipt of the German annuities, and the disposal of them to the various creditors, under the arrangements of Trust Deeds. But it had its origin in other considerations. Some of the creditors wanted it because they realised that unless international action were taken for stabilising gold, all this great scheme of debts and reparations might be brought to the ground. Such a bank would be the beginnings of real co-operation. The Germans wanted it because they said that unless some institution existed to

8

increase the credit of the world and its trade for the special benefit of Germany, they could not possibly extend their exports, not even to cover the annuities of the Young Plan. The annuities of the Young Plan for the first few years were considerably less than those for the Dawes Plan in the normal year, i.e. in the *money amount*, but owing to the fall in world-wide prices the real burden in debt soon became greater than it would have been under the Dawes Plan. Once more the real question of what Germany could pay was clouded by—what do the creditors owe? and the prospect of getting the German debt reduced below the figures of the Young Plan was very remote while those old war debts stood.

The French valued the Bank for International Settlements because they thought that it would provide the ready machine for enabling various public issues to be made, so that the German debts might be commercialised, and be due not from the German Government to a creditor government, but from the German Government or railways or some German enterprise to individual stockholders or bondholders in the different countries. They felt that this kind of debt could not be repudiated in any way without completely upsetting German private credit. This, then, was the stage reached by the reparations problem up to about two years ago.

All the great tussle at the Hague was not really to the point on the question of the amount that Germany should pay, but devoted almost entirely to relatively small questions, very distant in time, about the sharing of future payments. As a matter of actual fact, the sum due to England under the scheme was greater than the previous proportion under the old arrangement for the first ten years—after that up to the fifty-eighth year there were certain losses which, under a particular method of mathematical calculation, could be represented as a " burden " on this country. But to anybody who had a view of the limited possibilities of life in the Young Plan, it was obvious that the most important question was how much we should get during the maximum life of the Plan, say, a period of five or ten years.

After the Young Plan

The subsequent history is that of the collapse of the American lending power to Germany, owing to the American slump, and therefore bringing Germany right up against the necessity for producing an export surplus and getting it sold. This she did very manfully in the year 1930, when she actually exported a larger surplus than most people had thought possible, but she did it at great cost, for as prices fell the burden became greater and greater. The world-wide depression in trade and unemployment made the situation even worse. By the middle of 1931 it became quite obvious that Germany could not any longer go on with the annuities, and the Advisory Committee provided for under the Young Plan met at Basle in December 1931 and advised a complete cessation of German payments. (During the five years 1926 to 1930 the total deficits on the budgets in Germany were 220 million £, or almost exactly half the reparation charges during the period. The Advisory Committee said that it was due to the progressive deterioration of her economic life which led in due course to a falling off in revenue.) There was no agreement as to any further modification of the Young Plan. At the present moment it theoretically remains intact, though the privately expressed opinion in nearly every country regards reparations in the form in which we have known them in the past as practically a dead question. But it is so interlinked with the policy of debt payments and other political issues that no one can yet say what the next stage of this unhappy business may be. It seems clear to me that if the original scheme as approved by the officials and economists had been accepted, after allowing Germany, for a reasonable period, to accumulate working capital and get straight again, it is quite possible that such a debt might have been paid, and would have led to no concentration of gold in particular centres, and to no untoward circumstances such as we have recently seen.

Germany's Actual Payments

Clearly Germany has failed to meet even the modest taxation burdens imposed by the Dawes and Young Plans, seeing how considerable are her budget deficits. She equally failed, without foreign loans, to make payments abroad to cover her liabilities. In commodities she turned a balance against her of 90 million £ in 1924 to a balance in her favour of 40 million £ in 1926, and after 150 million £ on the wrong side in 1927, secured 75 million £ to the good in 1930. In the seven years, the adverse balance on commodity account was 315 million £. During this period she paid nominally 515 million £ in reparations, but she must have borrowed in one form or another 900 million £ to do it. In a period of five years she " transferred " 305 millions as reparations and borrowed 740 million £ from abroad. It was estimated that the net foreign investments in Germany at July 1931 amounted to over 1,000 million £.[1] It is small wonder that the situation is completely changed when the source of these loans dries up !

How much has Germany actually " paid " by now in reparations, assuming that all the money lent to her to do it is a good debt ? Up to the end of 1922 towards her " debt " of 6,600 million £ she was reckoned to have paid 275 million £. From the Dawes Plan to June 1931 she paid 502 million £.

The Fundamental Antithesis

There is no clearer indication than the history of reparations of the way in which monetary expressions cloak the real physical facts behind them, and if people realised the facts about the

---

[1] *Economist,* January 23, 1932.

transfer of goods from one national heap to another, they would appreciate the real underlying difficulties of the situation. If the production of the two heaps is very similar in its character, it is obvious that the creditors, those who draw from the heap to which additions are made, may care very little for the additions—they would much prefer to have other classes of goods —and the personal credit that they will give for these goods becomes mentally less and less. When this disinclination is expressed in price, it means that what they take off the other heap has very little extra value to them. If the subtraction from the German heap is put upon the heaps of other and neutral countries, it may well be that those countries who have to buy such additions will not wish to buy *also* the additions that would have been made from our own heap; in other words, the competition in neutral markets may be just as obnoxious to us as competition in the home market. The only way in which reparations could be satisfactorily paid in these days would be if Germany were the complement and not the rival of her creditors—were she an entirely agricultural and not an industrial country, or if she were an industrial country and her creditors were entirely agricultural. The influence of tariffs and of deflation taken together have been catastrophic in their effect upon the possibility of reparations on any large scale. The stupidity of democracies and the cupidity of political parties have combined to complete the wreck.

V

The Characteristics of Internal Debts

By " internal debt " we mean money borrowed by a government in the main from its own subjects, where what is paid by the taxpayers to the Government because of the loan is received by their own countrymen as interest, and what is paid by taxpayers for repayment is received back by people in the same country as repayment. Now, this is a mere interchange of parts of the national heap, for the tickets of ownership of production each year change hands when the taxpayer hands his ticket to the Government and they pass it to the loan holder as interest ; or when the Government pass more substantial sums to the loan holders, for these tickets of title to parts of future heaps, which we call the repayment of capital, also change hands. The whole process remains " in the family "—indeed, many people pass taxes from one pocket to another pocket as interest. It has been said for this reason that the problems raised by an internal debt are quite different from those of an external debt, for in the latter there is a natural subtraction from the heap which is taken right away, so that none of the people of the nation can enjoy it.

But there are two kinds of internal debt. There is borrowing for production and borrowing for non-productive purposes, such as war. In borrowing for production, the Government may be doing what a limited company might do—taking away the title to capital goods, bricks and machinery from individuals and then applying them to producing factories and increasing the size of the future heap to a greater extent than it would have been, just as individual capitalists may do. This is an increasing function of a government as it becomes collectivist or socialistic, or of municipalities as they undertake various trading and profitable enterprises. Borrowing for war purposes, however, even internally, obviously does not increase the size of the heap in future— whatever negative value it may have in preventing the heap from being much smaller through depredation from abroad—and it means that the taxpayer or the person who has borrowed, with nothing in return to show for it, has to give up some part of his title to the future heaps to the people who have lent the money at the time. The lenders may be sitting in idleness, and producing nothing in the future, because they are entitled to draw their subsistence from the heap.

It is often pictured that this rentier class are a great number of people who live in idleness upon the toil of others, so that if we could get rid of this internal debt, then not only would the payers

of the taxes—the payers of the interest, that is—
have more with which to enjoy themselves, and
a higher standard of life, but the recipients and
their heirs would have to set to and work and produce to place upon the heap at least the amount
that they themselves need to live upon for their
subsistence. It is easy to exaggerate the importance of this point, for most recipients have an
active occupation, and are already adding as
much as they are capable of, in any case. The
interest is an addition to their income, except in
the case of widows and retired persons.

The Capital Levy

A large internal debt is a great burden in the
sense that it is a burden upon the producers.
The whole idea of the capital levy was that this
effect for the future might be cancelled out. The
taxpayer was to be told that if he would give up
his title to a certain amount of future wealth
straightaway, and that were handed over to the
lender of the original money on loan to government, then he would be quit of the corresponding
future annual taxes or levies. To sacrifice £1,000
in capital in one lump was to be the same as
giving up £50 of income each year. To receive
£1,000 repayment outright was the same as
receiving £50 interest from the Government for
future years. The war loan holder would be
in possession of £1,000 stock in some company
instead of his war loan.

It would reduce the taxpayer's income, the

taxpayer's share, just the same, but the whole transaction would be got out of the way, and inasmuch as the person with a title to the heap in the future would also have to give up under the capital levy, that person was being made to pay his own repayment ; for war loan itself would be one of the most important items under the levy. This would mean that the war loan recipient would definitely give up a large part of his title to the future heaps. The extent to which he would be entitled to live on future heaps would be correspondingly reduced. The capital levy, it was said, did not annihilate any real wealth. All it did was to hand over certain tickets of title and tear them up. It redistributed the wealth, but it did not redistribute it in any different way from what taxation itself in future years would have done, except for the fact that the recipient of the taxation was himself liable. But the recipient of the war loan interest is himself liable to income tax on that interest ; and so the capital transaction —capital levy—was deemed to be an outright method of achieving what would have to be done year by year in future.

The Contrast with External Debt

The external debt was contrasted with this as being a definite subtraction from the national heap. As a matter of fact, there is little distinction from an economic point of view in the problems raised by the " transfer " and " export surplus " owing to external debt and those raised by reparations. One of the worst economic consequences of internal debt is the fact that it is expressed in money, and if money changes in value, the transfer of wealth from one class of owners to another varies very greatly. This is the way I expressed it when writing about it in the year 1920 :

The nation sees its fixed charges for interest and repayment of debt becoming a larger and larger proportion of its total income and resources. It borrowed from a man during the war what was equivalent to a pair of boots, and in ten years' time it finds it may have to pay back what is the equivalent of two pairs of boots.

This may be indeed no great hardship if the total production has so increased that two pairs of boots represent a smaller fraction of that total than one pair was at the time when the loan was made. To revert to our figure of the national "heap." If the heap remains approximately the same in actual goods, but the money tokens by which it is shared are fewer, the receivers of debt interest and repayment are entitled to the same money tokens, and therefore a larger and larger share of the heap. Only by the heap being made substantially larger as the money value of individual items diminishes can the actual proportion of it in physical objects which are transferred to these recipients be prevented from increasing. It is small wonder, then, that at the present moment we have a growing body of opinion that deflation is a wrong policy, and that we should try to keep prices somewhere about the present level. There are some who consider that we should not allow any material deflation until we have repaid a substantial part of the debt ; they say, with much force : " Let us pay back these lenders in the same kind of money that they lent us, for, if we do not, the burden will become intolerable." For example : a debt charge of 350 million £ a year, or, say, 270 million £ net, represents, out of a net national income of 3,500 million £, one-thirteenth part (say, 7½ per cent.) of the real products and services of the country. Now, when the money value of these services and products has been cut down to 2,700 million £, it represents one-tenth, or 10 per cent., and when that money value has got back to this pre-war figure, it represents more like one-seventh, or 12½ per cent.

I then showed that the average index number for the whole borrowing period was about 161, whereas the index number at February 1921 was over 200, and said that we should have to drop 40 points before we could be said to be paying back a greater value than we borrowed. And that position was reached in December 1921. I went on to say that the first repayments of war savings certificates were then falling due, and as the index number in 1916 was 136, we appeared to be innocently guilty of repudiation to the extent of some 6s. 6d. in the £. The very rapid and extensive deflation that has since taken place has, of course, completely altered this argument. When the Colwyn Committee were reporting on the same point, they said : " Despite a small decrease in the internal interest charge since 1919–20, the absolute burden measured in pre-war prices (wholesale) had increased by nearly 61 per cent. in 1925–6." But as the borrowing was in fact mostly prior to 1919–20, in that year " the interest receiver was suffering a reduction of his previous purchasing power." According to the evidence " a little over two-thirds of the debt may be regarded as having been raised when prices were above the present level " (1927).

The Present Weight of the Debt

Of course, the weight of the debt after the war, despite the fact that the price level index had trebled, was five times as great in capital, and (owing to the higher rate of interest) five times as great in the annual burden. Since that date we have reduced the nominal money amount of the debt by sinking fund repayment by over 400 million sterling, which represents a tremendous effort. And yet all this has really gone for next to nothing, for the interest and sinking fund payment was still over 350 million £ in 1931. And when we consider the real weight owing to the change in prices—what a picture ! In 1920 7,829 million £ of debt at the prices then was equal in pre-war values to 2,654 million £, and in 1931 7,413 million £ at 1931 prices is equal to 7,340 million £ pre war, or nearly three times as much, while the debt service is also three times as great as in 1920. The point of lowest burden was 1924, when 7,641 million £ stood at a level of 164. Let us call this a burden of 100. Then just before the great deflation in 1928, the burden became 114, and at March 1931 157. An addition of 57 per cent. to the 7,413 million £ of debt means that the effective weight of the debt in terms of 1924 values is 11,638 million £, or an increase of well over 4,000 million £.

Since March 1931 the situation has gone even

worse. I first expressed alarm at the prospect of deflation to the previous price level for this reason in 1920, both because of the relative weight of debt and the difficulty of raising enough by taxation out of the depressed profits resulting from deflation. In 1923 I pleaded for the level then existing as a fair compromise between the claims of the old and new generation of savers, and said that the pre-war price level would make a burden " too colossal for the nation to bear." In 1924 I declared that America would make the burden of our debt in production too high if she succeeded in forcing up the value of gold, and that she might very well carry it so far that Europe would be forced to get some kind of stability and trade revival without gold —to learn to do without it, and " gold would then from being unemployed become unemployable." [1] From 1928 onwards I have pressed home the increasing burden of the debt.

Of course, over a long period of years, if production, through the increasing power of science, becomes much greater, the heap may become so big that a stationary amount of goods to be transferred is a relatively small burden. If the population increases rapidly also over half a century, as in the nineteenth century, the war burden may also become negligible, but there is no sign yet of this happening. If it were not for the fact that the interest receiver and the taxpayer are to a

[1] *Observer,* 1924.

great extent the same person, and it is a larger instead of a smaller amount that is taken from the right-hand pocket to put in the left-hand pocket, it would be a very serious question indeed.

Debt Reduction by Conversion

But even without any change in prices, and solely through a change in the rate of interest, the method of conversion frequently relieves the annual payment at the expense of a much larger debt in future. For example, I may say that I will take over your war loan and give you instead war loan carrying a less annual interest burden, but promising you in repayment for every £100, say, £120 in sixty years' time ; then, although I do relieve the annual burden, I may increase the actual capital amount to be found some day by a considerable amount. And these increases in the final face value of the debt are a very questionable way of dealing with the total. A much more acceptable method is to take a promise to pay, say, 5 per cent. for the next thirty years, and exchange it for a promise to pay $3\frac{1}{2}$ per cent. for the next sixty. When the end of the thirty-year period is reached, if it is then possible to raise money at not less than $4\frac{1}{2}$ per cent., the Government by the transaction will have made a difference in the annual burden of 1 per cent. through its foresight. It is always possible to borrow money at a lower rate of interest than the normal, by promising to pay a larger capital sum on repayment than one has borrowed. This method takes two forms : (1) repayment at a premium and (2) borrowing at a discount. They are not essentially different in principle. The man who takes up £100 bonds at face value by paying £80, the bonds bearing 4 per cent., is really not different from the man who pays £100 for a 5 per cent. bond repayable at £125. But sometimes there is a difference in psychological appeal.

Comparisons

It cannot be stated exactly what is the relative burden of debt in each country, for that involves a precise knowledge of the national income or capital which is not available on comparable lines. But many calculations have been made comparing the burden of taxation. This is equally difficult, because the ideas of what to include in " taxation " vary so much, and what in some places is paid for by fees, or by ordinary commercial methods, in others may be covered by local taxes or rates. One calculation, least favourable to the position of the British, gave the percentage of national income represented by the tax burden in 1923–4 as 11·5 in the United States, 23·2 in Great Britain, 20·9 in France, 19·2 in Italy and 17·0 in Belgium. The League of Nations issued a computation in 1921 showing that as a result of the war Italy and Belgium had increased their *money* debt seven-fold ; France ninefold and the United Kingdom tenfold ; the United States twentyfold and

Germany fifty-eightfold ; but their real debts, after allowing for the changes in the purchasing power of their currency, were : Italy only 20 per cent. more ; France two and a half times ; the United Kingdom sixfold ; Germany threefold and the United States thirteenfold.

The three essential features in comparing the burden of two debts are the capital obligation to repay, the date at which repayment takes place and the rate of interest during the period. It is quite possible for two apparently very dissimilar burdens to be identical in actuarial value when they are reduced to present terms on a common basis ; and these three variants may be expressed in a way which will be attractive to particular individuals or trust companies, and yet, at the same time, yield a profit to the State. The art of debt conversion consists in turning one loan into terms of another in such a way that the individual will be prepared to make the exchange, while at the same time the State is making an immediate or ultimate profit according to its object. The reason for the difference is that the life of the State having no natural termination or horizon has qualities of expectation and ability which do not belong to the life of the individual. It may be that the individual does not mind much what happens after a period of twenty or thirty years in the next generation, and therefore he will be glad to take a slightly larger annual return with a complete cessation of the return at the end of that period, rather

9

than the lower return for sixty or seventy years, whereas the present value to the State may be very different in the two cases.

External Debt

Obviously, when we are considering external debt, particularly between two governments, much that would be reasonable or possible between the State and the individual is not possible between two States. The whole question of external debt is bound up in intricate international politics. The question whether the American debts to this country were really debts to our Allies, for which we merely gave them our additional credit, or the question whether they were really another way of America carrying on the war ; the point that they were debts incurred for materials bought at very high prices ; the later issue that repayment is difficult to the debtor because the creditor will not take it in the proper economic way in goods—all these are very well-worn topics with which you are quite familiar. The debtors distinguish sharply between this kind of indebtedness and the indebtedness for capital loans made in times of peace for productive purposes. The money has not been expended in any way which enhances national production and increases the national heap to an extent which enables the interest to be paid. It has all been blown away in shot and shell in unproductive ways, and can only be met out of pure taxation and not out of any increased yield. The recipients, on the other hand, the creditor states, rightly declare that they have borrowed the money from their citizens, and must repay it to them in any case. If they do not get it from the foreign debtor, then they must raise it by taxation of their own citizens. When we come to the way in which the debt has actually to be paid, then of course we are really in the field of economics.

Many American manufacturers have held for a period of over the last ten years that it is quite unnecessary for America to be incommoded either by gold or goods, for they can relend the money to the debtors. But this depends entirely upon the credit of the debtors, and their ability to make useful application of the money on a long-period basis. A continuous settlement by methods of relending is only a book-keeping repayment, and must some day find an end. One ingenious American writer says, both of reparation and external debt payments, that they can be relent to the debtors until the prosperity created in the debtors' countries is so great that they become natural exporters of surplus capital to the creditor, who then takes on the position of having a reversed balance of commodity trade left in his country. Over great cycles of years this operation of being alternately the country owing the money and having it lent back will, he says, settle the problem. When the Dawes Plan was being revised in Paris and the

Young Plan constructed, the European policy was, as far as possible, to identify and equate the debts they owed and the reparations they were to receive—a policy which the United States have never admitted. Germany protested that they could not judge her own capacity to pay and export goods, by the totally irrelevant consideration of the amount of money that the book-keeping of the Allies in the war had decided to say was due to America ; the two calculations had no organic relation whatever. While that is true, there is no doubt that in the actual payment of these sums they have a close economic relation, and in the outcome we find that America is by far the largest recipient of German reparations, through the medium, so to speak, of the book-keeping of the inter-allied debts.

The Burden of Debts Reshuffled

People have propounded various schemes for the more equitable division of the surviving war debts. I made some calculations showing that if all the existing debts had been pooled, and then divided out according to the average wealth of the countries, the United States would have to receive 1,461 million \$ from her four chief debtors in place of over 11,000 millions actually due to her. But that, of course, deals only with the accidental residuum for the war costs, which have to be left over undischarged out of individual taxation at the end of the war. If the different nations had contributed to the war

costs as a whole according to their respective
abilities, as judged by their national income,
the United States would have to receive 1,479
million $. But then again the United States came
late into the war, and if the war costs were pooled
as a whole for the war, and not merely from the
different dates when the nations came into the
war, then the United States on a " capacity to
pay " basis would have had to give up her
present debts altogether, and pay out to the
others a further ten million odd dollars. These
are just interesting speculations following out
logically the consequences of taking certain
principles.

When we speak to our American friends about
the money that we lent them in the nineteenth
century that they never repaid, they always
treat it, of course, as though we were discussing Egypt or Babylon—it is so long ago.
Well, of course, fifty or sixty years is a long
time in the life of a young nation, but on the
other hand the existing debts run for a period of
sixty years, and therefore there is some slight
parallel between them, and the repudiated debts
are not so prehistoric after all. During the fifty
years from 1830 to 1880 some twelve different
states at different times repudiated their obligations to countries and citizens. If we take the
face total of the capital so borrowed and the
accumulated interest at the date of the formal
repudiation in each case, and then work out
from that date at a fair rate of interest up to

the present time, probably the unpaid American debt to this country would exceed 250 million sterling. If we took also all the smaller munici-palities and cities as well that repudiated their debts, and accumulated them at compound interest, not at an ordinary rate, but at the *actual rates of interest that were promised on the bonds*, we might perhaps reach a figure of from 400 to 500 millions sterling.

The reasons why we were unable to recover our debts is a matter of history. But it is a curious comment upon the Federal constitution which would not let us take political action for our debts and would not recognise them itself. In four years after repudiation the twelve states which owned a quarter of the national wealth added to their own wealth sufficient to pay twice over every dollar of the defaulted debt.

Sinking Funds

In State borrowing the most attractive loans have of course sinking funds attached to them, and the history of sinking funds is a very interesting one. For a long time the British Government were practising an absolute fallacy on this subject. They thought they were really providing a sinking fund, when all the time they were borrowing an equivalent amount in other directions. It is a cardinal feature with State finance that no matter how closely tied up to a loan it may be, except for the security of that particular loan, a State is not really providing a sinking fund at all unless it has a surplus of taxation over current expenditure. Complicated and ingenious borrowing devices do not get over this fatal dilemma.

The burden of internal debt is an extremely heavy one in this country. The burden of the debts from Napoleon was also very heavy ; it was about one-third of the national wealth, but by 1914 the national debt was less than 5 per cent. of the national wealth, despite the additions that had been made by the Crimean and Boer Wars.

Recapitulation

Now let me recapitulate.

First : The economics we have been trying to study are not a mass of facts so much as a mode of thinking. I have tried to make you see behind all statistics and forms and figures the realities of the movement of goods and the claims of individuals to use them.

Second : During war the "heap" may be increased in all countries, but a large part of it is taken for war uses, and only a minimum left for consumption for non-war purposes.

In the third place, the sales of existing claims to share in foreign heaps, which we call sales of foreign securities, enable large additions to be made to commodities for the purposes of war.

Fourth : Less of the heap is devoted to repairs and renewals of the fixed assets that are not consumable year by year, but which help, with human labour, to increase each annual heap.

Fifth : Foreign borrowing gives a new title to the production existing on the other national heaps, with an undertaking to replace in peace-time in years to come the amount so taken.

Sixth: The proportion of the national heap taken away from individual consumption and devoted to war purposes is accounted for in three ways. First, the compulsory transfer under government action, which we call taxation. This is outright and extremely fair as a method, but it is generally limited in the extent to which it can be carried out by the psychology of the people because it impairs their incentive to produce, and limited, too, by the administrative machinery necessary for carrying through equitably devised individual taxation.

In the second place, the transfer takes place by borrowing, or, as we call it, throwing the burden on the future, in the sense that people yet unborn, who would be otherwise compelled to produce for the heap before they could take from it, will inherit a right to take products they have not themselves made, but which have to be made by other people still unborn. There is no immediate inequity in this, because if one person spends all he has after paying his taxes, while another denies himself and saves, the second one is certainly entitled to some different treatment. Moreover, apart from war-time and war loans, people who are thrifty

or wish to provide additional income in various
ways make other kinds of investments, and it
would be exceedingly unfair to penalise those
who put their money into war loan as distinct
from those who put it into a business. The mere
cancellation, therefore, of war debts would be a
complete injustice to one set of individuals as
compared with another. The capital levy was
not applied in time, or at any rate, during the
period when it would have been justified by
economic conditions. But the stage when it was
most justified was the time when it was least
practicable, because of the tremendous movement of prices and the impossibility of carrying
through the valuation upon which it would have
to rest.

The third method of securing a large proportion of the heap for war purposes is inflation,
which is a kind of very uneven taxation. We
have seen that inflation leads ultimately to a
collapse of the whole price system, or to repudiation by the State, or other borrowers, of their
debts, or ultimately, to severe deflation and
consequent trade depression. One of the three
must inevitably follow.

Seventh : Apart altogether from national action
in these three respects the whole world is indulging
in gold deflation, which is very serious in its effects
upon society, on all debts and reparations whether
political or commercial. This inability to control
gold as the basis of value is the fundamental
cause of all our depressions.

Eighth : Next we saw that reparations must be paid either in goods or in loans, and that loans must also be paid in goods *some day*. Then we saw that external debts were a subtraction from national production and not very different in their economic effects from reparations, whereas internal debts were a redistribution of goods—a redistribution of the national income.

Ninth : Running through the whole of our discussions has been the fact that *money* is the real variable, whereas we are in the habit of regarding it as the thing that is fixed. Even when we fully appreciate that it *is* the variable, we act as though it were not. We make all our elaborate calculations for transactions of all kinds on the tacit assumption that the money with which we are doing it—the gold, the dollar, or whatever it is in which we express it—means the same thing throughout the whole period of our contract. In the second place, when it obviously does not behave in that stable way, we insist on going on as though it had done so—as though there were no change in the burden ; as though the distribution of income were just as equitable and just as fair. We arrive at a wage settlement which we think does justice to capital and to labour, and in doing it we assume that the money in which it is expressed will have a constant purchasing power. When we find that this assumption does not turn out to be true, instead of recognising the fact that it is not true, and making the appropriate adjustments, we pretend to each other and we try to persuade each other that it has been, and that no case exists for varying it. We talk of the sanctity of interest, or the impossibility of lowering wages, and thus by the two mistakes, first of all assuming that no variations will take place, and then refusing to recognise that a variation has taken place, we bring ourselves wellnigh to the verge of destruction.

Tenth : The root mischief as regards the reparation problem is that *no responsible body has ever been given the task of determining the total Germany is able to pay* in production of goods and services. This problem has *escaped*, contrary to popular impression, between the meshes of the following :

(*a*) The Treaty decided the *kind* of things that Germany ought to pay for.

(*b*) The Reparation Commission decided *how much in money* the items under (*a*) came to.

(*c*) The Conferences said how (*b*) *ought to be spread* over different years.

(*d*) The Dawes Committee revised (*c*) for a period of years *on an export basis*, but had to leave the total of (*b*) untouched.

(*f*) The Young Committee cut down the total (*b*), not on a production basis, but to the limits of certain *money debts due by the creditors*—a variable and uncertain burden of goods not related to Germany's capacity to pay.

No one has therefore been allowed to ask or to

answer the question, " What can Germany rightly spare from her national heap and what will the others take ? "

.   .   .   .   .

I think two things will have emerged in the minds of all of you, and whatever else you may forget, I hope that those two will stay. The first is the need for stability in money values. The second is that the mere monetary expressions and statements that we make on all these financial questions are not in themselves anything real or final ; they can only denote a movement of goods and services with human effort behind them, and it is that human change that we have to keep our eye upon. Every time we should ask the question : " What is happening behind all this façade of monetary expression ? " If we once learn to do that, then the mysteries of these financial proceedings, following upon the tremendous disruption of war, will at last begin to have a semblance of reality for us all.

APPENDIX

The gold standard is a fairly modern device, and silver has served the purposes of the world for a much longer period in history. We left silver for gold in the nineteenth century ; we led the way, and other countries followed us until all except Eastern countries, such as India and China, treated gold as the measure of the values of things and services. Everything has a " value " measured in other things ; thus 1 lb. of tea may be worth 5 lb. of sugar in exchange, or 1½ lb. of butter, or an hour's work in the garden, or a 'bus ride from London to Windsor. But it would be very awkward if tea in a grocer's shop had to be marked with all these different prices or equivalents, and still more awkward if it could be bought only by bringing one of these equivalents to the shop, and just the one the shopkeeper happened to want. For a number of excellent reasons mankind, though it has used cubes of tea, furs and other articles as measures of value or price, and as the ready means of buying and selling, has settled down on the precious metals as best adapted for the purpose. They do not rust or rot, and they can be divided without loss, and carried about. So the value of a cwt. of tea came to be expressed in a certain weight of gold, that weight being conveniently referred to in a number of uniform pieces or sovereigns. If shillings were used for small transactions they were merely convenient legal substitutes at the rate of twenty for each sovereign, and large debts could only legally be discharged in sovereigns. Now, particular things are worth more than others, largely because they are harder to produce, and 1 lb. of tea is worth 5 lb. of sugar mainly because the trouble or work in getting these quantities is equal. If it suddenly becomes much easier to get sugar, the price of tea might be 10 lb. of sugar instead of 5. It would be the same with the price of tea in gold, which, let us say, is £10 per cwt. If the price changed to £20 per cwt., it might be either because tea was much harder to grow or because gold was much easier to find and to mine.

Why Prices Fluctuate

In the simplest terms, the quantity of money or gold determines prices. And this is one of the drawbacks of the use of a physical object like gold for money—it may vary very much in its quantity or ease of production, and therefore affect all the values which it measures. So if a money payment is fixed in amount, it may buy much or little at different times. Now, this has actually happened in practice, and gold has varied in its value in other things widely over a space of, say, twenty-five years. Generally speaking, when new gold has been easy to get, through new mines, it has been less valuable, and more of it has had to be given for other things, so that their price has risen, although nothing has happened to the production of those other things. For the price of a thing is its equivalent in gold, and that is the first essential of a gold standard.

People think, naturally, when the price of a thing rises or falls that it is due to something changing in the demand for, or supply of, that thing. So it may be, but equally it may be that the thing has not changed at all, but that something has happened to gold, for which it is in effect being exchanged. But people find it very hard to think of price in this way. We know that the sun does not go round the world daily, but that the world spins on its axis, yet instinctively for ordinary purposes we regard the earth as still, and the sun as " rising " or " setting " and moving across the sky. Now you will see that, price being the equivalent value in gold, it is very dependent upon the quantity of gold compared with the quantity of other things. And this relationship by quantity is all-important in the working of the gold standard.

I have talked of it in its simplest form. But gold may no longer circulate, and, instead, pieces of paper, each representing so much gold in the possession of the bank or country responsible for the paper, have the same effect. The number of notes would correspond exactly with the gold, and an additional note could only be issued if additional gold were put in the vaults. So the quantity of gold is still linked with prices payable in notes. The next stage is where a certain number of the notes are not exactly represented by actual gold, but all above that fixed number are. This is the British case. Again, since the notes in circulation are always more than the unbacked quantity, in fact notes are not added without equivalent gold being obtained. All countries are not on the gold standard in precisely the same way, for in some the notes have to have a minimum percentage of gold to represent them. But in all of them the quantity of gold is important. Of course, payments are made and debts settled within a country by other means, cheques, etc., but in the long run the total money of whatever kind used in a country has some definite relation to gold, either by law or practice, so that more gold, more money and higher prices ; less gold, less money and lower prices. This is a main function of the standard— to set an outside limit upon the creation of money and credit, and put it beyond caprice or human frailty and political desires. The price of gold in notes or coins is fixed by law. There used to be the right for everyone to turn gold into sovereigns and back again, without limit, but this is not an essential feature.

An International Guarantee

I now pass to the second feature. The prices of goods exchanged between countries, though expressed in dollars, francs, sterling, marks, all mean the same thing in gold equivalent. Every merchant and trader knows exactly where he is in quoting and accepting prices abroad, for, whatever currency he gets, it is translatable into the others by their common relation to gold. This is an immense convenience, for if one currency has not a permanent price in another it is difficult to buy and sell for long contracts, owing to the risk of a change in the relative values of the moneys during the period of manufacture or contract.

A third feature is that gold is the means of settling differences in the accounts between nations. If England buys 20 million £ worth from Germany and sells 10 million £ worth, then, unless Germany is prepared to lend us indefinitely the difference, we have to export gold to balance the account. As we have no gold mines in England, we can only obtain that gold by selling to gold-mining countries our goods and services to earn it. Gold is a commodity, in international trade, but it differs from all other commodities, for it is agreed upon as the universally accepted commodity for balances. If we had a tea standard, all our prices would be quantities of tea, and whenever a trade balance had to be met between two countries a quantity of tea would have to be sent.

10

Automatic Controls

Now, the gold standard is really a sensitive piece of mechanism, mainly because of this relation between the quantity of gold and prices. A ball-cock is a mechanism in a cistern, keeping the water at a particular level. A thermostat comes into action by cutting off the supply or escape of heat when certain limits of heat are touched, and keeps the temperature at a constant range. So the gold standard is, under proper conditions, a device which keeps the international trade of the different countries properly paid for. Let me illustrate one or two of the ways in which it performs its correcting or equalising functions. Suppose that all the individual traders of country A (without, say, one individual knowing it or controlling it) sell 100 million £ of goods to separate individuals in country B, and those in country B sell 50 million £ to A. Assuming there are no other countries to bother about, B owes 50 million £ on balance to A ; A does not propose to lend the money to B, but wants it for its own spending and income. Then, by the processes of the exchanges, it will be settled by 50 million £ in gold getting transferred from B to A. So the quantity of gold in A goes up, and since money and prices in A are related to gold, prices begin going up and A becomes an attractive place for B to sell in (for B's costs have not gone up), and thus more goods tend to flow from B to A. At the same time, the quantity of gold in B has gone down, and money and prices tend to go down, so that B becomes a poorer place for A's traders to send their exports to, and the flow of goods from A to B tends to fall. Now, when prices fall money wages can fall to correspond without altering real wages measured by goods purchased, so that a fall in prices in B is reflected in lower money wages and costs, and makes B able to export more cheaply than A. And, correspondingly, in A the rise in prices and money costs makes A less able to export to B. So you have four influences at work to alter prices. These make two changes in the flow of goods. They reduce A's power to export below 100 million £, and increase B's power to export above 50 million £. The tendency is now for the accounts to balance without the export of gold from B to A, and the influences set to work tend to go on until the real gold prices in the two countries reach equilibrium again. So the gold standard acts as a powerful corrective to " unbalanced " exchanges of trade, and tends automatically to prevent countries buying " on tick " for very long. (There are all sorts of other conflicting circumstances which there is no room to introduce here, and we cannot look at the process in individual detail to see how the buying and selling of bills of exchange make the gold flow when imports exceed exports.)

Now, take a second aspect of this self-adjusting device. One of the levers attached to it is the bank rate. When gold is going out of a country, the bank can defend its reserves by offering a higher rate of interest on money than other countries are doing, so that balances and deposits tend to remain with it on loan. This prevents too great a contraction in the amount of its money and reduction of its prices. This is preventing the equilibrium process from acting, and obviates the correction by borrowing. But the higher bank rate makes home business harder to do profitably, and by employing fewer people restricts business. This lowers money wages through competition for employment. This also reduces prices through costs. This, again, makes the country less favourable for others to sell in, and makes it better able to compete abroad with its exports, so this all tends again to equilibrium between exports and imports.

Equilibrium Upset

This is the theory of the gold standard, and also the way in which, in the past, it has really acted. But you will see that it really depends upon certain things happening inevitably and automatically. If money does *not* increase for any reason when gold comes in, prices do not go up, and our thermostat fails to work automatically. If when gold goes out, prices and money wages do *not* fall, the assumptions underlying the correction do not exist, so that the automatic corrective tendencies are not set up, and the gold standard fails to act according to theory. Now, there have been, since the war, several elements

present which prevent these fundamental
assumptions from being facts. First, if the total
production and the total gold available as the
basis of money remain reasonably matched, then
world prices will remain fairly stable, and prices
in individual countries will fluctuate closely
round world prices, controlled, as I have
indicated, in the scope of their fluctuation. But
if any large part of the gold gets into a position
where it is no longer used as a basis of money,
the effective world stock of gold becomes less,
no longer matches production, and world prices
must fall. So, if a flow of gold takes place to
particular spots, and is lost so far as its influence
on money and prices is concerned, then prices
do not rise there and the gold standard mechanism does not act. Now, such a flow of extra gold
has taken place to France and America, and it
has not been allowed, for reasons no doubt good
in those countries, to have its natural effect on
prices, which could have increased their imports
and diminished their exports. But the drain of
gold from other countries has lowered their own
price levels, and thus lowered also the world
level. The corrective motions of the gold standard have been jammed. Features antagonistic to
the smooth working of the standard are : the
heavy " one-way traffic " of debts due to
America, which tend to be receivable mainly in
gold because imports of goods are impeded by
tariffs, and the desire to prevent a national rise
in prices because of the risk of speculation and

inflation. Similarly, the standard presupposes a fluid, or at any rate supple, response of money wages and costs to changes in price (though it does not presuppose any marked change in real wages), and if money wage payments do not readily move up and down and the wage structure is rigid, as it is in this country, then the standard is jammed again. When gold prices fall, if costs in the export trades do not go down, the export trades cannot expand to correct the adverse trade balance. At the same time individual purchasing power to obtain imports is not sufficiently reduced, and so the foreign trade exchange remains unbalanced and gets worse. The standard does not work. At the present time we are spending at the rate of one hundred millions abroad more than we are selling, and we used to be two hundred millions the other way round which we could lend.

The Ultimate Choice

It is correctly said that the standard involves personal inconveniences for the greater general good, and that different countries have not been willing to concede things that they do not like. The standard has been rightly said to unite all for good or evil in a great international partnership conferring benefits, but imposing on each stern duties, so that deviation by any one from the general rules reacts on all. The Macmillan Committee said it was only workable if all agreed upon their aims and co-operated to bring them

about. I do not here describe all the advantages
of the standard, or the drawbacks of its destruction because of the non-acceptance of its rules,
nor the kinds of alternatives, nor its place in our
present troubles. I have merely tried to set out,
in a way rather different from the textbooks,
those essentials of the standard which have had
most importance in recent times.

There is no moral question necessarily involved
by these obstructions. That it would be better
on balance economically to give up particular
national practices and desires that obstruct, for
the general advantage of a smooth-working
international money standard, I have no doubt
or hesitation about. We cannot have both our
separate national desires and also the advantages of the gold standard. Something has to be
given up, and the world has to decide which is
better on balance.

The way it works is not a moral question, and
it is no more use preaching sermons to it than to
a locomotive. You may blame a locomotive for
not doing more than it was designed to do or
ever mechanically able to do. That is ridiculous
morally. You may blame it for not doing what
it is theoretically capable of doing, when you
have really messed about with the works. That
is absurd morally, too. The more you know
about the gold standard mechanism the less
sense is there in using the term " bankers'
ramp" about recent events. When a car refuses to
climb a wall or go one hundred and fifty miles an

hour, or let you go to sleep, you might as well talk of a " drivers' ramp."

The nations together are giving the gold standard an impossible job to do. Devise a better machine or improve the machine, but it can still only work according to the limits set by its own constitution, and not how you would like it. The gold standard is not worked merely by bankers ; everybody, politicians, workers, employers, all unconsciously take a hand, and a special attitude of any section or nation may make it unworkable. There is nothing political in this—it is bare economics. Our object must be to maintain a standard, internationally, which will go on working and producing price stability, despite folly and ignorance and sectional disadvantage, for the general good.

REFERENCES FOR FURTHER STUDY

I

1. STAMP : Fundamental Principles of Taxation, ch. iii.
2. STAMP : Taxation during the War, chs. ii and vi.
3. STAMP : Current Problems : The Capital Levy.
4. STAMP : Wealth and Taxable Capacity.
5. Colwyn Committee on Taxation and the National Debt.
6. HARVEY FISK : British Public Finance.

II

7. LAYTON : Money and Prices.
8. LEHFELDT : Money.
9. Dawes Report on Reparations, Part II. Also (4) above.

III

10. Macmillan Committee on Currency and Finance.
11. STAMP : Gold and the Price Level.

IV

12. KEYNES : Economic Consequences of the Peace.
13. KEYNES : Revision of the Treaty.

14. MOULTON & MCGUIRE : Germany's Capacity to Pay.
15. STAMP : Report to International Chamber of Commerce on Reparations.
16. McFADYEAN : Reparation Reviewed.

V

17. HARVEY FISK : British Public Finance.
18. STAMP : Criticism and other Addresses, xvii, xx.

Printed and Made in Great Britain by
Hazell, Watson & Viney Ltd. London and Aylesbury